T96.3

DATE DUE			
NOV 19 1991			

MITTS

MITTS

A Celebration
of the Art of Fielding

WILLIAM
CURRAN

WILLIAM MORROW AND COMPANY, INC.
NEW YORK

Library of Congress Cataloging in Publication Data

Curran, William, 1921–
    Mitts : a celebration of the art of fielding.

    Includes index.
    1. Fielding (Baseball) I. Title.
GV870.C87   1985   796.357'24   85-2897
ISBN 0-688-04489-1

Printed in the United States of America

First Edition

1 2 3 4 5 6 7 8 9 10

BOOK DESIGN BY CINDY SIMON

In memory of my mother and father

Acknowledgments

On occasion the novelist or short-story writer, nestled in his air-conditioned aerie at the console of his word processor, can create a work while drawing solely on God-given resources. Never so the nonfiction drudge, daily dependent upon others to fuel his muse—librarians, historians, editors, mailmen, deponents, shopkeepers, friends and acquaintances, idlers on street corners, and senior citizens on park benches. Under such circumstances, it may never be possible to recall and cite all persons who contribute to the making of a book like this. But let me try.

Sincerest thanks to:

Tom Heitz, librarian at the National Baseball Library in Cooperstown, New York, and his eternally helpful staff assistants, Jeff Kiernan and Donna Cornell.

The staff of the Seattle Public Library, which must have one of the country's most resourceful and courteous telephone information services; no query of mine, however outrageous, has yet been met with hesitation or even a small gulp.

Paul MacFarlane, historian at *The Sporting News*, who does not always agree with my assessment of old-time ballplayers but who is unfailingly generous in sharing his colorful recollections of "the way it was."

Anonymous but kind and helpful reference assistants at the Library of Congress, the University of Washington Libraries, the New York Public Library, the Harvard University Library, and the Kitsap County (Washington) Library.

John Kuenster, editor of *Baseball Digest*.

Bill Deane for sharing information on the development of fielding and permission to quote from his article, "The Best Fielders of the Century," which appeared in the 1983 edition of *The National Pastime.*

Arnold Hano, who did virtually grow up at the Polo Grounds as we would have liked to.

Red Barber, whose counsel in matters of baseball comes as close to profundity as any is likely to.

The Rawlings Sporting Goods Company and the Spalding Sporting Goods Company for sharing with me materials from their files.

Dozens of former major-league players, managers, coaches, club executives, and baseball writers who generously replied to my letters and telephone queries.

Equally helpful colleagues from the Society for American Baseball Research (SABR).

Mark Rucker for his invaluable help in gathering photos.

George Cole and Jim O'Donnell for bringing their considerable baseball know-how to bear on the manuscript in its embryonic stages.

Shirley Curran and my children, Bruce, Nancy, Barry, Neus, and Courtney; and also Barbara, Valerie, Lauran, and Bryan Cole; and Georgia Cole Bamber for what is often described by the pallid term "moral support," but is very much more.

And finally my editor, Jane Meara, and my agents, Sherry Robb and Bart Andrews, for assistance so varied that it defies cataloguing.

As that fine catcher and admirable human Yogi Berra might have expressed it, thank you all for making this book necessary.

Contents

"There is a sweet spot in time for catching a ball just as there is for hitting one."
JOHN JEROME
From *The Sweet Spot in Time*

"Skillful fielding is by all odds the most attractive feature of the national game."
HENRY CHADWICK
"The Father of Baseball"

MITTS

ONE

Before the Gloves Turned Gold

"Babe Herman's glove would last him a mini-mum of six years . . . it rarely made contact with the ball."

—FRESCO THOMPSON

BEWARE, YOUNG BASEBALL FAN, THE OLD GUY with the kindly face and ready smile, who slips quietly into the seat next to you just before they play "The Star-Spangled Banner." He will shake his head in disdain as the visitors' lead-off man beats out a swinging bunt toward third. You may hear him mutter, "Ossie would've had that in his hip pocket," or "Pie would've cut him down by three steps." Don't ask who Ossie and Pie were. He's sure to tell you before the fifth inning.

By the time the home team has gone down in order in

15

the first, already trailing by two runs, the old-timer will make an effort to strike up a conversation. If you don't respond, he may content himself with a monologue. He will proclaim to the night air that ballplayers sure aren't what they used to be. Not on your tintype. Why, fifty years back, batters were not only sharp-eyed, they were paragons of discipline. Hardly ever went for a bad pitch. Well, maybe Ducky Medwick. But he used to drill waste pitches for doubles. There was Joe Sewell—four whiffs a season. Imagine. And Lloyd Waner—most umps would delay the call until they saw what "Little Poison" thought. Real hitters, those guys. Look at the averages. Lefty O'Doul hit .383 one year and got lost in the pack.

Once wound up, the old guy will assure nearby fans in Section EE, a small tear forming in the corner of his eye, that in that lost, sun-drenched world, countless young giants lashed blue darters to all fields off right-handers and southpaws alike. Cheetahs in human form churned the base paths and kept inviolable the deepest reaches of the outfield. Pitchers? Utterly brave and tireless. Listen, son, a guy would throw a shutout in the first game of a doubleheader, then race to the bullpen to stand by to save the nightcap. Yes, sir, that's the way it was. Then, all of a sudden—it was maybe the fifties—something went wrong.

At this point your grizzled neighbor may pause to order a hot dog, or whatever septuagenarians eat at the ball park. In guarded tones, lest the vendor overhear, he will confide that he suspects a residual influence of Dr. Spock. Or the Warren Court. Possibly the widespread fluoridation of the drinking water. No matter the cause. The sad fact is that the once happy fan now finds himself saddled with a lot of pampered multimillionaires who bat .230 in a good year and hire personal hair stylists to accompany them on road trips.

Hear the old fellow out, young fan. It's a matter of courtesy and you may even find him entertaining. But don't for one minute believe what he says about today's game. In general, the big-league player of the 1980s is bigger, smarter, faster, stronger, better educated, better nourished, and, above all, better instructed than his counterpart of fifty years ago. I have seen both generations perform, and while I hesitate to declare openly that today's players are innately more talented than those of the 1930s, the evidence suggests it is so. Be assured, in any case, that the only giants loose on the diamond fifty years ago wore orange and black socks with low stirrups and played at New York's Polo Grounds. They were fun to watch and I cherish the memory, but my conviction is that all but a few—Mel Ott, Bill Terry, Carl Hubbell, Travis Jackson, and one or two more—would risk being blown away in today's high-powered game.

Nowhere is the disparity in performance between the generations more apparent, I think, than in improved fielding and defensive strategy. The 1930s never knew a shortstop with the range and precision of an Ozzie Smith, a Mark Belanger, a Dave Concepcion. The best of the old crowd, and here we may be talking of four or five, would show up in today's game as hardworking journeymen. I would say that the same is true for the other positions, with the regrettable exception of first base, still too often turned to as a sanctuary for the inept of hand and heavy of bat.

Oh, yes, I know that to express such a view is to call down wrath upon my aging head. It has happened already. On every hand I confront angry protestations that "it's the gloves. It's those newfangled, cavernous, Venus flytrap gloves. Any idiot can field a thousand with a bushel basket strapped to his wrist." Hysterical voices remind me that today's playing surfaces are like pool tables even when they are grass, that official scorers are weak-kneed and spineless, and that the coddled Gold Glove outfielder scarcely ever has to play in sunlight as his disadvantaged grandfather had to do.

It's hard to understand those who readily concede that fielding today in the majors is a lot better than it was fifty years ago (the evidence is irrefutable) but insist that reasons for the improvement must be sought in anything but the natural superiority of the modern player. In every other sport the continuing improvement in performance is acknowledged without question. Modern swimmers are faster than the old-timers. The clock proves it. So are runners and skiers. Football, basketball, and tennis players are more skillful than their grandfathers. Just look at some old game films. Why not baseball players?

Unquestionably, the modern baseball glove is a marvel of design and construction, a great convenience to players at all levels. But there will never be a substitute for having a skilled hand inside the glove. The fact is that the best-quality gloves of the 1930s were very well made and could hardly be viewed as a handicap to the good fielder. The real revolution in glove design had taken place way back in the early 1920s.

In any case, the style of glove used by any player in any era is a matter of personal taste, and that taste can vary widely. Joe Morgan, an outstanding fielder, uses a glove that would make many 1930s models look oversized. Baltimore Orioles fielding wizards Brooks Robinson and Mark Belanger also preferred relatively small gloves. Red Sox outfielder Jim Piersall, a phenomenal ball hawk of the 1950s, used an infielder's glove. So it goes.

Speaking of personal taste in gloves, I recollect having seen only two old-timers' gloves close-up. One belonged to the New York Giants' Bill Terry, the other was Joe Di-

Maggio's. Terry's first baseman's mitt can best be described by saying that if a housewife discovered it lying on her back porch, she would beat it with a broom and scream for help. DiMag's glove looked like it might have been fashioned from one of the Dead Sea scrolls. It was folded vertically down the middle and appeared in danger of cracking in two if opened any wider than was necessary to have someone's bid for a triple disappear into the fold. If there was any difference between the condition of the leather of Joe's glove and that of the scrolls, I would say that the glove was a bit drier.

Would Terry and DiMaggio, two of the most brilliant fielders in the history of the game, have performed better if they had been equipped with giant, 1980s, state-of-the-art gloves? Improvement would have been hard to measure—the two were that close to perfection. By the same token, there are still a few guys loose in the majors today—home-run hitters, of course—who couldn't be counted on to corral the ball with a custom-built trawling net.

What about the claim that it is mostly the difference in quality of playing surface that makes today's player appear a better gloveman than his predecessors? Well, I'm not going to argue with Brooks Robinson when he tells me that artificial turf can "make you feel invincible." But at present only ten of twenty-six parks are blessed (cursed?) with a rug. Elsewhere, the moderns face the same grassy hazards that their grandfathers did, perhaps more, if truth be known, since the old parks were less frequently chewed up by professional football teams and never by rock concerts.

Allowing for the veil of romance through which it is so tempting to view the past, the major-league fields of the 1930s that I saw close-up were beautifully maintained.

True, I was just a kid and saw only a handful. But common sense tells me that during the Depression, when labor was abundant and cheap, there was no excuse for a major-league team not to keep its field in top condition.

To satisfy myself on this point, I asked Dick Bartell, a scrappy little shortstop with the Phillies, Giants, and Tigers in the 1930s. "The playing conditions were good," he said. "I don't know of any infield I could be critical of with the exception of Saint Louis. Cincinnati was a bit hard at times. But Saint Louis was the worst. And even that wasn't so bad."

I don't doubt that back in the last century, some major-league fields were little better than cow pastures. You see evidence of it in old photos. But even in those days there must have been some decent ones. The old Baltimore Orioles employed a full-time grounds keeper. So did Chicago. The point is that when a fielder drops a fly ball that's right in his glove, or uncorks a wild throw, it doesn't matter whether he's standing on a rock pile or Astroturf.

I don't want to create the impression among trusting youth that there were no outstanding fielders in the 1930s. There were some great ones, as there are in any era. I've already mentioned Terry and DiMaggio. Add to those Mel Ott, Al Simmons, Bill Dickey, Mickey Cochrane, Charlie Gehringer, Billy Herman, Bill Jurges, Stan Hack, Sammy West, Kiki Cuyler, and I could probably name a dozen more. But my recollection is that reliable fielding skills did not reach down through the twenty-fifth man on the roster, as is more likely to be the case today. And, in general, the attitude toward defense seemed much less intense than it is now; at least it appeared so from the stands.

Memory can play tricks, I know, but I could swear that fifty years ago almost any medium-speed ground ball back through the pitcher's box was sure to go for a single. As a kid I would start to mark my scorecard before the ball had passed the rubber. In the outfield, lazy fly balls regularly dropped between lead-footed outfielders as batting averages soared. And fans sitting in the box seats behind first were in greater danger of being hit by an infielder's throw than by a line-drive foul.

Until the last thirty years it was almost a convention for infielders and outfielders alike to put on weight in the first flush of prosperity and lose some of their range and quickness. That doesn't happen much these days, and when it does the offending gourmet finds himself facing heat from the front office and a schedule of weigh-ins. Too often a speedy outfielder of the 1930s was condemned to cover twice his normal territory because the manager had stationed some tortoiselike slugger on his flank. On occasion a general manager's fantasy of new home-run records would bring together three behemoths in the same outfield. The only record broken would be triples by the opposition.

If fielding was less than distinguished a half-century ago, it was very much worse in the early 1900s, and unimaginably bad in the last century. Consider that in the championship playoff of 1885 between the National League's Chicago White Stockings and the St. Louis Browns of the American Association (then a major league), the teams made *one hundred errors* between them. Chicago, led by the legendary Cap Anson, booted a cool seventeen chances in the seventh game, which, it will not surprise you to learn, they lost. These clubs were the league champions. Picture, if you dare, a playoff between the tailenders of 1885.

Through the whole evolution of baseball, one fact stands forth with abundant and irrefutable clarity: Fielding skills have followed a consistent upward curve. Batting, pitching, and baserunning have all registered ups and downs, but fielding just keeps getting better. The phenomenon is acknowledged by baseball historians (regardless of the causes they may assign) and recognized informally by senior citizens of any era who have been steady and impartial patrons of the game.

Listen to the eyewitness testimony of "Candy" Cummings, originator of the curve ball and winner of 124 games over a period of four seasons back in the 1870s. Martin Quigley, in that charming book *The Crooked Pitch*, describes an occasion when, after a long absence from the game, Candy was taken to see the Red Sox at Fenway Park. The season was 1921. "It was not the pitching but the perfection of the fielding that impressed Candy most," Quigley writes. "'It's too perfect,' he said of the errorless play. 'Errors are part of the excitement. It wasn't like this when I was pitching.'" You bet it wasn't. During Grant's administration, fifteen errors a game was routine.

Dallas Adams, an Australian-based baseball statistician, has devised with the aid of a computer a highly complex measure of relative pitching and fielding skills and the differences between modern players and those of earlier times. He traces a steady, almost inexorable advance in fielding from the first days of the professional game, allowing at the same time for such variables as improvements in equipment and playing conditions.

He writes:

> On the fielding side there has been a dramatic and nearly continual overall improvement. A large part of this, especially in the early years, is likely the result of improved baseball gloves and better playing fields. Nevertheless, fielding

over the past decades, in conditions of modern gloves and groundskeeping, also shows a fairly steady improvement.

Any comparison of quality of play between one generation and another is necessarily based on the record and supplemented by random judgments from long-lived fans and baseball writers. It's about as exact a science as government economics. But it's the best we have.

Every baseball fan learns at an early age that numbers, such as batting averages, fielding averages, and a pitcher's won-and-lost totals, tell only part of the story. The acrobatic stop by a third baseman just inside the line, or an outfielder's leaping catch against the 440-foot marker, looks in the record book like any other assist or putout. One of baseball's oldest clichés is that the base-clearing pop-fly double in the seventh inning resembles a line drive in the box score. And what fan has not seen a pitcher add to his win total with a 15–9 outing while an unhappy teammate yields only three hits in the nightcap and loses 1–0. It's the reason that statisticians like Bill James are constantly seeking new measures of performance.

A classic instance of how unannotated stats can mislead the unwary is the distinguished fielding career of Henry "Zeke" Bonura, who played a casual first base for the White Sox and the Senators in the 1930s. A ponderous, good-natured fellow, scion of a well-to-do New Orleans family of fruit importers, Zeke swung a lethal bat and could be counted on to drive in a hundred or more runs a season. He was also a .300 hitter. On the other hand, his footwork around the bag would not immediately bring to mind Fred Astaire or Mikhail Baryshnikov.

Year after year, when official fielding averages were

published at the close of the season, fans who had watched Zeke play would gasp to find his name leading all American League first basemen. In fact, Zeke was charged with only sixty-eight errors in his playing career, a sum which the average first baseman of the Gay Nineties would have matched in a couple of seasons.

How did Zeke manage such commendable stats? Well, let's say that he was a zealous disciple of Cap Anson's "lamppost school" of first-base play. You could count on him to come to grips with any throw that was zeroed in on the middle button of his size-48 blouse. But let a toss be a foot or two wide of the bag, and Zeke would be stunned into immobility. His disapproving eye might follow the flight of the errant throw into the dugout or the right-field bullpen, but never would he break faith with his beloved base. And as for ground balls, Zeke would as eagerly grapple a king cobra as put his glove in the path of a hot smash.

Maybe my recollection of Zeke's play is not properly tempered with compassion. Maybe his spirit was wholly committed to cutting off all those two-base hits down the line, but his 220-pound bulk refused to respond to its airy dictates. Besides, when you bat .330 and drive in 138 runs, why be concerned about dinky ground balls from the bats of .240 hitters? One thing is sure. When baseball historians of the twenty-third century examine the musty records, Zeke Bonura will be indistinguishable from Hal Chase or Keith Hernandez.

As general managers are wont to point out to .350 hitters at contract time, raw numbers can sometimes be deceptive. But before we abandon conventional stats and risk turning Howard Cosell's toupee dead white, let's take a second look. Despite their shortcomings, standard baseball records—batting, pitching, fielding, and baserunning—still tell us a lot about how well the game is or has been played. Their value has been established for more than a century, and that's why organized baseball and ancillary agencies are willing to spend much time and money to amass them. The trick, of course, is in how they are interpreted. It's only then that mere box scores are turned into statistics.

Baseball writer and analyst Bill Deane, who has done extensive research on major-league fielding records from 1900 to the present, reminds us that the value of the numbers lies in what is revealed by the *large sample.* "Over a period of time," Deane writes in his essay "The Best Fielders of the Century," "we will usually find that the players considered by their contemporaries the most dominant at their positions consistently emerge among fielding average leaders. It is not coincidence when a Brooks Robinson wins eleven FA titles or Luis Aparicio eight. So, despite its flaws, FA is still the most useful statistic we have for measuring defensive performance at all positions."

Deane's findings are reinforced in a sense by the work of Professor William E. Akin of Ursinus College, who has devised a system for assessing the quality of fielding in the nineteenth century. He writes, "As every student of the game knows, fielding stats are less than exact measures of a fielder's quickness, range and arm, but over a decade they usually indicate clear patterns."

I belong to a wonderful organization called the Society for American Baseball Research, also known as SABR. My impression is that many of my SABR fellows own computers and daily engage in wizardry with baseball records, which threatens to revolutionize the way player performance is evaluated. I expect to wake one morning and hear that a SABRmetrician has demonstrated beyond question that Rex Barney was the best control pitcher of his generation. It is rumored that general managers tremble and agents for .220 hitters smile every time a SABRmetrician sits down at his console. No cow remains sacred within earshot of his humming machine.

Unhappily, I do not yet own a computer, and if I did I doubt that I could manage anything more challenging than my checking-account balance. SABR keeps me well supplied with such esoterica as Base-Out Percentages and Strikeout Differential Proficiency. I am and probably must remain just an old-fashioned baseball fan. Nevertheless, I can still read a form chart. Let me explain.

Not long ago I was working with *The Baseball Encyclopedia*, a volume that has not replaced the Bible on my night table, though it seems to have nudged the Good Book back toward the Kleenex. I figured out that in the 1970s, twenty-four major-league teams—twenty-six for the last three years of the decade—were guilty of 27,644 errors, playing schedules that ran 162 games. It works out to an average of 1.74 errors per game for the decade.

To allow for a span of half a century, I compared the figures with those for the 1920s, a period beyond my personal experience. I learned that back then, two eight-team leagues, playing schedules of 154 games, managed 32,180 errors, or an average of 2.61 bobbles per game throughout the decade. What it means statistically is that if in both decades you had leagues of equal size playing schedules of equal length, the old-timers would boot 15,000 more chances than the players of the 1970s. Think of it—15,000 more fly balls dropped, throws into the dugout, ground balls through the infielders legs in the same number of games. That's a lot of errors to charge to small gloves or lumpy infields. I felt vindicated.

In one of his many books, the late Fred Lieb, who may

have covered more World Series games than any writer in history, observed that Giant outfielder Fred Snodgrass's costly dropped fly in the final game of the 1912 Series could be charged to simple carelessness. In the 1926 Series, the Yankees' usually reliable left fielder, Bob Meusel, was similarly guilty, and it cost the New Yorkers game seven and the winner's share. Of course, anyone can make an error, but if teams as well disciplined and rich in talent as McGraw's Giants and Huggins's Yanks could be guilty of major lapses in concentration when all the chips were on the line, what must have been the attitude toward defense of lesser teams in those days, especially in unpressured, midseason situations. I think the record book is eloquent on the matter. And please don't tell me about the gloves or the hardhearted scorers. When a fly ball pops out of the pocket of a man's glove, there is only one way you can score it. In substance, the scoring rules have not changed in 110 years.

Fred Lieb's comment about Snodgrass has always stuck with me because it reinforced an impression I carry of baseball before World War II. I think a lot less heart went into defense then than does today. There seemed to be a kind of Alfred E. Neuman spirit abroad. If, for example, Zeke Bonura played an easy roller into a four-base error with men on (yes, he really did), you could imagine the players saying, "Not to worry, guys. We've got five regulars hitting over .330. We'll get it all back in our half." And often they would.

Oh, it was a different world and a different game. I confess that with all its mechanical imperfections, I loved watching it. The air in those sunlit old ball parks seemed to be filled with flying baseballs. Even reserve catchers hit a ton, and if you saw a ballplayer with a worried look, you knew he was a pitcher.

For the fans it was heaven. Fly balls that didn't drop for extra bases between lumbering outfielders often crunched against outfield walls in those cozy old parks. After a line-drive hitter like Chuck Klein or Paul Waner had been through town, grounds keepers would spend two days cleaning up shards of concrete from the warning track.

In an interview with Lawrence Ritter in the 1960s, former Washington Senators slugger Goose Goslin recalled the happy agony faced by hitters back in the thirties. "Jeez," he said, "you had to be a wizard to come anywhere close to the top in those days. A guy who hit .350 was considered just an average hitter." Goose was scarcely exaggerating. In 1930, the Phillies' regular lineup batted a collective .343. Of course, the same lineup allowed the opposition almost 1,200 runs in 154 games. But, what the hell, the other guys were entitled to their share of the fun.

And wondrous things could happen afield on almost any day. Frenchy Bordagaray, a perennial free spirit and sometime outfielder for the Brooklyn Dodgers, was pursuing a long fly ball one afternoon when his cap flew off after the manner of Willie Mays's. To show you how priorities can shift in half a century, Frenchy first went back to retrieve his cap and then continued after the ball.

I once saw Cincinnati's gargantuan catcher Ernie Lombardi hit a 450-foot line drive at the Polo Grounds and become victim of a triple play. It would take pages to detail the imaginative base running that contributed to this event. But it really happened.

Lombardi's feat pales slightly when matched against what happened to the Red Sox's Joe Cronin a season earlier. With the bases loaded, Cronin hit a cannon shot in the direction of Cleveland's third baseman, Odell "Bad News" Hale. The line drive caromed off Hale's skull into

the hands of shortstop Billy Knickerbocker, thence around
the horn for a triple play. Hale never was quick with his
glove, not even in self-defense. Some years later, I saw
him duck in the nick of time to avoid being crowned by a
two-out infield pop-up. Three runs scored.

Do not think for one minute that Hale and Bonura performed in haughty isolation. There were many who shared
the act—the incomparable Smead Jolley, Rudy York,
Hack Wilson, Bob Johnson, Dale Alexander, Lefty
O'Doul, Moose Solters, the aptly named Boots Grantham.
Only protective amnesia prevents my naming dozens
more. Jim Levey was known to create the impression that
the St. Louis Browns had puckishly installed a croquet
wicket at shortstop. At Philadelphia's Baker Bowl, it was
said that the right-field grass had more pockmarks than an
artillery range from the fly balls that dropped without hin-
drance around the Phillies' Buzz Arlett. At Cleveland's
League Park, a dugout wag who had just muffed an easy
chance in left field alibied that Indian outfielder Moose
Solters had left the area contaminated by his bad play.
Visitors were being infected.

Any saga of creative fielding must begin with the name
of Floyd Caves "Babe" Herman, the only player ever to
draw his unconditional release when he was batting .416.
It seems that on the only day the owner of the Omaha club
could get out to the park to check his team, Babe tried to
field a pop foul with his head. Over the frantic protests of
the manager, who did not have an abundance of .400 hitters, the choleric owner shipped Herman off to yet another of his many stops in the minors. Babe played for
eighteen clubs before he reached Brooklyn and immortality.

From my own experience in watching Herman, I must
say that he was anything but uncoordinated. How can a

guy bat .393 against big-league pitching and be uncoordinated? He had pretty good speed when compared with
most outfielders of his day, and a good arm. The problem
seemed to be that Babe did not always have his head in
the game, especially when batted balls were on the loose.
It was widely suspected that he was busy calculating his
batting average through the last turn at bat.

In a game at New York's Polo Grounds in the mid
1930s, I saw Herman—he was then with Cincinnati—
stand in short left field fondling the ball as he watched the
winning run score from second in the bottom of the ninth.
It should not have been surprising. He had been involved
in similar lapses in the past; in one he left the field with
the ball after making the second out of the inning and let
the base runners circle the bases unchallenged.

On the very next afternoon the identical situation pre-
sented itself. The Giants had tied the score with a two-run
rally in the ninth and had the go-ahead run on second. The
Giants' Hank Leiber drilled a line single to left which was
in Herman's glove on one quick hop. The base runner
could not have been halfway to third when Babe came up
with the ball. But instead of throwing home, he spent several seconds authenticating the signature of league president, Ford Frick, jammed the ball in his pocket, and
headed for the clubhouse in center field.

When Cincinnati manager Chuck Dressen had been suc-
cessfully restrained from homicide, suicide, or both, he
slapped Herman with what I recall was a two-hundred-
dollar fine. In those Depression days it must have had the
sting of two grand for one of today's players. It was
rumored that the Babe never did understand what the fine
was for.

Maybe you think I exaggerate about the Thumping
Thirties. I acknowledge that the mists of fifty years may

cause some mild distortions, but not much. Recently, I came across a piece by the late Tom Meany that reinforces my recollection of the spirit of the age. Commenting on Brooklyn Dodger manager Max Carey, Meany, who spent some harrowing years covering that team for several New York newspapers, wrote, "He had hopes for '33, provided he received some help in the shape of an outfielder who could hit and was an even-money bet to escape with a whole skin in a duel with a fly ball." Then Meany goes on to report that Carey's hopes finally settled on the person of young Joe "Poodles" Hutcheson, who was the size of an NFL tight end and had demolished minor-league pitching with his fifty-four ounce bat. Young Joe opened his major-league career like a human tornado, driving in an average of three runs a game. He was also letting in about two runs a game with his lead feet and Teflon glove. Not to worry. The balance was still in Brooklyn's favor.

The problem started a couple of weeks later when Joe's hitting cooled a trifle. He was only driving in about one run a game. But he maintained his accustomed pace in the field. Not long after, Hutcheson was back, powdering the ball for Amarillo or Ottumwa or wherever he had come from. When you consider that the kid was playing in the same outfield with Lefty O'Doul and Hack Wilson—and just missed sharing the field with Babe Herman—it makes you wonder if Carey wasn't a trifle harsh in his judgment.

I ought not to dwell on the old days. Nostalgia threatens my sense of proportion. I find myself wanting to jump aboard a time machine to get back to the early thirties in time for a doubleheader between the Dodgers and the Phillies. Today, with a couple of men on base, you hit a grounder anywhere near Ozzie Smith, Alan Trammell, Manny Trillo, or any one of a dozen of these human vacuum cleaners, and what do you get? A killjoy, inning-ending double play. Hit one fifty years ago in the direction of Lonny Frey, Lou Chiozza, or Odell Hale, and the odds were pretty good that it might be the start of a seven-run rally. And if you think that the old-time fielders were generating all this fun unaided, consider that in 1936 American League pitchers had a combined ERA of 5.04.

Sometimes it's hard to comprehend that a generation of players whom I look back upon with affectionate disdain were viewed by Candy Cummings as magicians with gloves. What must the game have been like half a century earlier with guys like Pete Browning, Cap Anson, Bill McClellan, and Frank Fennelly on the loose? The record book offers a hint, though we must remind ourselves that it's only part of the story. In 1887, for example, the American Association fielded .905 as a league and the New York Mets (yes, Mets) contributed 643 errors in 133 games. That's nothing. The association had pulled itself up from a mark of .884 in 1883.

In 1901, its first year of existence, the American League posted an undistinguished .938. But clearly fielding was headed in the right direction. By contrast today twenty-six major-league teams field a collective .980. That's astounding. It's the average of a top-flight outfielder of fifty years ago, a superstar of 1920.

Like others of his generation, the old fan in Section EE senses that the game is no longer what it was in his youth. Or in his father's youth, for that matter. He's right. Principally, the fielding is a whale of a lot better.

TWO
Batting's Handmaiden

"There's more to this game than hitting."
— FRANKIE FRISCH

IN THE BEGINNING WAS THE BAT. WELL, MAYBE IT was the ball. But I'll bet you that when some Cro-Magnon fashioned the first crude ball from an oak knot wrapped in antelope hide, his pal in the next cave was already eyeing a stout limb on the nearest ash tree with a thought to taking a swipe at the new plaything. As Trevor Bailey reminds us in his fine history of cricket, "There is something challenging and fascinating about trying to hit a ball that has been thrown, which has always appealed to man and still does."

Ancient man must have worked off some of his natural urge to bash things by combining it with the need to hunt. Can't you see our hairy ancestor holding his Alley Oop club way down by the knob and happily taking his cuts at rabbits, wild goats, maybe an occasional woolly mammoth? Alas, progress, often a mixed blessing, brought agriculture with its more dependable, but tranquil, methods of obtaining food.

What about the bashing impulse, ever at flood? Was it to be gratified by such passive surrogates as mosquitoes, parlor rugs, or erring wives? No. A man needed a target that would send a tingle through his forearms, something challenging. And that's why at the near end of the evolutionary chain we find a society addicted to whacking golf balls, tennis balls, squash balls—but especially baseballs.

If you review the history of baseball's probable antecedents—rounders, one-hole cat (now one o'cat), early cricket, town ball—one fact is immediately evident. These are hitters' games. Not only did the batter (in town ball called the striker) dominate the game, he was the game. The sole function of the pitcher (appropriately known as server in town ball) was to satisfy the needs of the striker. Then, as now, the striker's need was chronic—a nice, fat, off-speed toss about waist high. And finicky hitters were known to sniff at up to a hundred pitches before being tempted to swing. Their prerogatives were built into the rules.

In these early games, fielding must have evolved from the dreary necessity to retrieve a batted ball from the tall grass. A congenital rulemaker may have been driven to propose ways of getting the bat from the hands of the insatiable hitter short of knocking him down and tearing it from his grasp. And so we had a system of outs. Out on three (or more) missed swings, out on a fly caught on the first bounce, out on a caught fly (rare), or out after being hit by a thrown ball while running between bases, called plugging or soaking. At last the ragamuffin in the field had a share in his own destiny.

But rules are rarely a panacea for the oppressed. In town ball, for example, it was imperative to win the coin toss for first turn at bat, since the bottom of the first inning might not come until the following day. It was not unusual for the team at bat to score hundreds of runs before being forced into the field when some cretin let himself become the third out.

I don't doubt that the lads in the field were honing their skills. But improvement was slow. As many a tyro has learned in Little League, the mysteries of the fly ball are not unraveled in a fortnight. Town-ball rules were eventually changed so that the winner was determined by which team could first score a fixed number of runs, usually one hundred. Now the toss for first at-bats was, in effect, the ball game.

When, in the 1840s, Alexander Cartwright and the young gentlemen of the Knickerbocker Club devised and codified the game we recognize as baseball—carefully measured rectangular diamond, foul lines, sack bases— they went even further than the earlier games toward establishing the batter as uncrowned king. Where the server in town ball had been relatively free to throw in any way and at any speed he chose, in the new game the pitcher was enjoined to do exactly that—to pitch (lob the ball underhand). His duty, in Cartwright's words, was to "serve the bat." In fact, it became the custom in baseball for the batter to tell the pitcher precisely the kind of pitch he wanted and to wait without penalty until he got it. Reggie Jackson, you were born a hundred years too late.

The pitcher wasn't the only one playing under constraints in Cartwright's game. For an outfielder to make a special effort to snag a fly ball and so deprive the batter of "his pretty hit" was held to be unsporting and would likely have fetched some early-day Willie Mays a word of censure from the club president.

As has been the fate of numberless institutions sprung from the mind of a gentleman, Cartwright's Sunday pastime suffered changes from the moment the working classes put their roughened hands to it. Bricklayers took it into their heads that the purpose was to win the game, not simply to play it for the sport. A blue-collar pitcher no longer saw his role as the compliant server of home-run balls to a spoiled batter. His job was to get the bum out. Inevitably, the hitherto indolent fielders joined the conspiracy.

Before you shed a tear for the gentleman batsman and his circumscribed wagontongue, be assured that he maintained one hell of a strong lobby among baseball's rulemakers (and still does). If new attitudes about winning operated as a spur to pitching and fielding in the 1850s and 1860s, you couldn't tell it from the scores. In 1859, for example, in the first intercollegiate baseball game on record, Amherst beat Williams, 73–32. The game didn't even go nine innings. Actually, the well-coached and gifted collegians were engaged in a pitchers' duel compared with the more typical game of the period. Usually, scores resembled something out of the NBA.

Not even the pros were exempt. On their highly publicized western trip in 1867, the Washington Nationals, nominally amateurs though every player was carried on the federal payroll as a "government clerk," scored 532 runs in their first 6 games. Two years later, when the Cincinnati Red Stockings, the country's first openly acknowledged professionals, made their historic tour, star shortstop George Wright batted .518 in 52 games. He scored 339 runs and hit 59 homers. Since outfield fences were unknown, a share of Wright's homers were probably ordinary drives that rolled between torpid fielders.

Evidence of the way fielding skills tended to lag behind batting can be seen in Henry Chadwick's description of the "muffin squad" in 1876. Chadwick, baseball's first sportswriter and record keeper, widely honored as the "father" of the game, wrote: "A player may be able to hit long balls and to make home runs, and yet for all that be a veritable muffin, from the simple fact that he can not field, catch or throw the ball decently." We still have our contingent of muffins. But today we call them designated hitters.

George Wright was no muffin. There's a story that he used to thrill crowds with a pregame exhibition of throwing the ball high in the air and actually catching it. And Joe Start, the New York Mutuals' first baseman in the early 1870s, won the nickname "Old Reliable" not because like the Yankees' Tommy Henrich he could be looked to for an extra-base hit with two out in the ninth, but because he could be counted on to catch *most* of the balls thrown to him. Jack Chapman of the Brooklyn Atlantics, one of the few outfielders of his generation who could consistently catch fly balls, was hailed in sporting journals as "Death to Flying Things."

Whole libraries have been written on batting techniques, but very little on methods of fielding. Among the earliest on record is the "New York style" of catching the ball, which was popular in the period before the Civil War. It was more often called the clamshell. You guessed it: The player would hold his wrists together, palms open, fingers outstretched, and reach for the ball. Ouch! Back in

the 1850s, Monday mornings in summer must have meant a crowded schedule for bonesetters and manicurists.

As a matter of fact, the clamshell survived well into the twentieth century. Before World War II it was much in favor with girls' softball teams—with predictable results. Ah, but the lasses were charming in their pleated, white flannel skirts, middy blouses, and saddle shoes. Today, of course, our Valkyries of the diamond spear line drives with the one-handed insouciance of an Amos Otis.

Fortunately, among nonmuffins of the last century the clamshell appears to have been short-lived. It was superseded by a second New York style, a relaxed, soft-handed cupping of the ball—much the way a player today would accept a throw bare-handed. This technique may have been the most significant advance in fielding before the appearance of leather gloves in the late 1870s.

Until the Civil War, clamshell stylists were spared some punishment by a rule that permitted them to retire a batter by catching his fly ball on the first bounce. In a game between all-star teams from Brooklyn and Manhattan in the late 1850s, twenty-seven batters were retired on the one-bounce rule. It would be interesting to know how many of the remaining twenty-seven simply struck out. As late as 1882, a batter was out if his foul fly was taken on one bounce. Catchers must have hated to see that one leave the books.

How did our forefathers do at tilting with ground balls? Evidence is scanty to nonexistent, but there is no reason to suspect that they outshone Lonny Frey and Zeke Bonura. Look at the scores.

We can make a mistake, I think, in lavishing sympathy on the gloveless heroes of the last century. Except for catchers, men in the field probably didn't have it rough until the late 1870s. We know that up to the Civil War and beyond, the catcher played well behind the plate—estimates vary from twelve to fifty feet—where he could take the pitch on a bounce. It's a clue to what pitching speeds must have been. It also means that the ball wasn't coming off the bat very fast. We know, too, that until late in the century, most batters gripped the bat with hands spread apart and tried to "push" the ball in a predetermined direction rather than belting it with a wrist-snapping full cut. Few infielders were getting knocked down by line drives.

In spite of allowing themselves a safety zone, catchers took a beating. With two strikes on the batter, the more intrepid ones would move closer to the plate to be in a better position to catch a foul tip. Often their reward was a split lip or broken nose. Some took to wearing broad rubber bands around their mouths in an effort to save lips and teeth. The bands must have helped, because George Wright's sporting-goods company began to manufacture them. The development of gloves and masks in the late 1870s may have slowed carnage among catchers, but to this day it has not ended entirely.

Pitchers were not finally freed from the requirement to release the ball from below the waist until 1884, but an 1872 ruling permitted them to throw as hard as they wished within these limitations. They no longer had to lob the ball, and trick pitches, such as the curve ball, were tolerated. The 1872 rule quickly helped to spawn the first generation of pitching superstars, men like Boston's Al Spalding, Philadelphia's Dick McBride, and Chicago's George Zettlein. Increased pitching speed meant that the ball was coming off the bat faster. That posed problems for the men in the field, especially for the pitcher himself, whose handsome features were initially only forty-five feet from the plate. It's no surprise that the use of protective leather gloves spread rapidly in the 1880s.

With the introduction of the curve ball and the appearance of gloved fielders, guess who was starting to feel the pinch? You know it, the man with the wood. To make matters worse, in 1875, after five years of experimenting with balls of different degrees of liveliness, organized baseball adopted for general use one called the Ryan dead. It was enough to cause a slugger to sit down on the bat rack and cry.

In point of fact, hitters suffered little. A good share of them continued to bat over .300, a few over .400. But never again would they know the delirium of George Wright's .518. More significant from the standpoint of fan interest, there was a revolution in game scores. The 103–21 charade of the 1860s was gone forever. Scores of 4–1 and 5–3 became commonplace. Maybe the fielding had improved somewhat, too, although a league FA of .866 makes you want to ask: Improved from what?

Inevitably, the unthinkable happened. The powerful Chicago White Stockings went a full nine innings without scoring a run. The news was flashed to a stunned nation and, for a time, a shutout became known as a Chicago. Baseball had come full circle.

On the heels of the dramatic changes in the character of the game during the decade of the 1870s, the rules committee in the next twenty years issued more edicts than a United Nations commission on Third World prerogatives. Scarcely a year passed in the 1880s and 1890s without a major shift in the playing and scoring rules. Most seemed designed to curb the growing power of the pitcher and to guard the ancient rights of the batter.

The pitcher's box, the area in which he could maneuver as he delivered the ball, was reduced over time from a roomy six feet by six feet to the point where they had the poor hurler anchored to a twenty-four-inch-by-six-inch rubber slab. He's still there. The pitching distance was increased from forty-five feet to fifty feet, then to sixty feet six inches. Almost yearly, the number of balls required for a walk was reduced, dropping from nine to four between 1880 and 1889. On the other hand, batters were permitted to use flat-sided bats.

In fairness it must be acknowledged that what the rules committee was clearly seeking was a proper balance between batter and pitcher. Since the game had developed into essentially a duel between these two, balancing their strengths could only make it more interesting for the fans. A couple of rule changes actually went against the batter, although it is shocking to note that not until 1901 in the National League and 1903 in the American League did a foul ball count as a strike against the batter. Imagine what that little concession must have meant to nineteenth-century sluggers like Dan Brouthers, Pete Browning, and Ed Delahanty. Over time, of course, the rules committee came through with flying colors. What emerged was the finest team game ever devised.

Through the flurry of rule changes, fielding, always baseball's stepchild, was largely ignored. Each position player was left to work out his proper function through trial and error—mostly error. In 1876, for instance, the first season for the newly formed National League, the New York entry booted 473 chances in 56 games for a slick .825 FA. That was nothing. In subsequent seasons, some teams would post more than 600 errors.

Maybe as early as 1874, the baseball establishment had learned the unwisdom of meddling with fielding. In that year, the National Association experimented with the use of a tenth man in the field—a kind of roving shortstop, like the shortfielder in slow-pitch softball. That idea was abandoned after just one season. You can put fifteen men in the field, and if none of them can catch the ball, you're no better off than you are with nine. Besides, adding extra men to the lineup only cuts down on the number of at-bats each player gets. Who could be happy with that?

Subsequent rules and recommendations affecting fielding have been uniformly negative, mostly being restrictions on size and style of gloves. Through the 1880s and 1890s there was much fulminating about the need to preserve baseball's "manly style" (a favorite term of Anson's), by which was meant slugging. Competent fielders were no doubt viewed as a threat. In 1888, George Wright, the greatest fielder of his generation and himself a manufacturer of gloves, advocated restrictions on their use lest they put hitters at a disadvantage.

Maybe the general policy of neglect by the rules committee actually freed fielders to continue to improve. Way back when the baseball fathers abolished the one-bounce rule, they forced fielders to confront the physics and metaphysics of the fly ball. On the whole, players dealt with the conundrum of fly balls admirably, though a few would argue that the process is still going on.

Contemporary accounts confirm the suspicion that until the 1890s the greatest single shortcoming among fielders was immobility. It was particularly true of infielders. Following custom, they clung to their bases regardless of what was going on. No first baseman or third baseman would dream of deserting his base to charge a bunt. Some, like Anson, felt that bunting was a contemptible little maneuver anyway. Bunts were best left for the pitcher. He didn't bear the responsibility for guarding a base. There was also an inclination among infielders to shun fly balls as though the play had been designed by the Almighty to be handled by an outfielder.

A few players with outstanding defensive skills began to build a following among fans, just as hitters and pitchers had done earlier. Understandably, catchers were among the first to attract attention. The Giants' Buck Ewing, Detroit's Charlie Bennett, and the St. Louis Browns' Doc Bushong became as popular for their glove work as Buffalo's Dan Brouthers and Louisville's Pete Browning were for their booming bats. Jack Glasscock, who played for several National League teams, was acclaimed "King of the Shortstops," and Cincinnati's second baseman Bid McPhee was believed to have no peer at handling grounders, unless it was Chicago's Fred Pfeffer. There were favorites at other positions, too: Chicago's Ned Williamson at third, the St. Louis Browns' Curt Welch and Philadelphia's Jim Fogarty in the outfield, and the Browns' Charlie Comiskey at first, to name a few.

SABR member and veteran Cub fan Emile Rothe, who has studied extensively the early days of organized baseball, reports that newspaper accounts of the 1870s were likely to praise outstanding fielding plays over other aspects of the game. Maybe it was because they were rare.

The big change in fielding just before the turn of the century was the final abandonment of the habit of immobility. St. Louis's quick-thinking first baseman Charlie Comiskey, who later achieved fame as a manager and owner, is often credited with pioneering the new style. He was first to dare to play well off the bag and move with the play. He also taught the pitcher to cover the bag on a ball hit to the first baseman. When Comiskey first reported to St. Louis in 1882, he caused Browns fans to gasp by racing back into short right field to take pop flies.

Baseball historian Harold Seymour argues that imaginative infield play antedates Comiskey. Nevertheless, it was Charlie who first attracted attention and sometimes drew censure. One day when the daring "Commy" was playing off the bag, a St. Louis writer asked a colleague, "How does Comiskey expect to take throws from Latham and Gleason [Browns infielders] when he's standing out there in right field?"

If Comiskey, or perhaps some forgotten predecessor, originated flexibility in the field, it was Ned Hanlon's Baltimore Orioles of the 1890s—Hall of Famers John McGraw, Hugh Jennings, Willie Keeler, Wilbert Robinson, Joe Kelley, and company—who brought the idea to fruition. When Hanlon, a former Detroit and Pittsburgh outfielder, took over as manager late in the season of 1892, the Orioles were dead last. The following season, Baltimore fans were treated to a sight never seen before. As described by historian Robert Smith, whenever the ball was hit:

> Every man on the Baltimore team would shift position at top speed, just as if they all worked on intricately connected and invisible cams. If the ball was hit to left, the third baseman would scamper out to the grass to get ready to assist relaying the ball back to the diamond. The shortstop would move toward third base. The second baseman would hustle to his own bag. The center fielder would sprint over to be in position to recover the ball if it got away from the left fielder. Even the catcher and the pitcher would scramble to get into position to stop possible overthrows.

The Baltimore strategy was bewildering, sensational. But it worked. Combined with new tactics in batting and baserunning, it inaugurated a style of play known as inside baseball.

Under Hanlon, Baltimore reduced its season's total of errors from a stupefying 584 in 1892 to a more fashionable 293 by 1894. In the process, their fielding average went from the National League's worst to the best, and they moved from twelfth place to first in the standings. While winning three pennants, they also created a legend. To be sure, the success of the old Orioles was not due entirely to their improved fielding. They were one of the league's best hitting teams, and they enjoyed good, if not outstanding, pitching. But the improved glove work certainly helped.

The lesson of Baltimore was not lost on others. Inside baseball was universally imitated, and for the next twenty years teams were content to play for one run at a time and hold narrow leads with the help of good pitching and tight defense. The revolution of the sound glove had triumphed. The day of the five-hundred error season was gone forever.

Don't get the idea that the beleaguered hitter just dried up and blew away in the face of this doughty defense. In 1899, for example, the National League, still at twelve teams, batted a very respectable .282, and Washington's Buck Freeman belted twenty-five home runs, a mark that was not bettered until Ruth hit twenty-nine in 1919. In its first year of existence, the American League in 1901 batted .277, which shows that they were not starved for base hits either.

For reasons having little to do with glove size, playing surfaces, or even the reformed drinking habits of left-handed pitchers, but possibly a consequence of the new foul strike rule, hitting began to decline in both leagues after 1903. To make matters worse, in 1905, Fielder Jones's Chicago White Sox, stigmatized by the second worst team batting average in all baseball, handily defeated their hard-hitting townsmen, the Cubs, in the World Series. The shocking victory of the "hitless wonders" raised fears that a team might need little hitting to win if it had good pitching and a sound defense. Predictably, the disciples of ash were quick to raise the cry for affirmative action for batters.

Typical was the proposal in 1908 by Francis Richter, editor and publisher of the influential *Sporting Life*, that outfielders be stripped of their gloves to make amends to the hitters. Fortunately for the welfare of the game, the rules committee disregarded Richter's recommendation. On the other hand, they did grant his wish indirectly by introducing in 1911 the lively, cork-centered baseball. Yet even with this historic assist, hitting continued to suffer fits and starts until after World War I, when it is rumored that more rabbit was added to the ball, and Babe Ruth and colleagues were able to rewrite the record book. Babe demonstrated that the gloves hadn't been the culprits after all.

Speaking of Ruth and gloves, it's worth pausing to remind ourselves that many of the same guys who were pulverizing the new ball—Ruth himself, Joe Jackson, Tris Speaker, George Sisler, Edd Roush, Eddie Collins, Nap Lajoie, Zack Wheat, to name just a handful—were among the outstanding fielders in the game as well. There sometimes is the risk in discussing hitting and fielding of seeing them as tasks performed by different species of animals. Perhaps animals is not the wisest term to use when speaking of hitters; make that creatures.

Concurrent with the Ruthian revolution in hitting, fielding in both leagues continued its steady improvement, though it's doubtful that anyone noticed, least of all the fans. They were much too busy watching balls fly out of the park. In 1925, the *New York Tribune*'s acerbic W. O.

McGeehan summed up popular attitude toward defensive baseball. "The perfect baseball game," he wrote, "if it could be ballyhooed in advance, would not draw a corporal's guard."

Acknowledging, as always, that fielding stats tell only part of the story, the part that they do tell is well worth looking at. Below are some records from the turn of the century to the outbreak of World War II, a period of great fluctuation in both batting and pitching performance. Here you can see the steady advance of fielding skills. I have included league fielding averages by decade as well as seasonal averages of errors and double plays.

	NATIONAL LEAGUE			AMERICAN LEAGUE		
	FA	E	DP	FA	E	DP
1901–1910	.955	2,030	761	.954	2,277	728
1911–1920	.963	1,877	881	.960	1,982	865
1921–1930	.969	1,551	1,069	.968	1,582	1,143
1931–1940	.971	1,414	1,139	.970	1,428	1,196

I am most impressed with such isolated facts as that the American League made 2,875 errors in 1901 (and fielded a shameful .938), and by 1940 had cut their errors in half. I'm sure that few fans and probably no players of the 1930s were aware of it. Who has the time or inclination to check fielding averages when an entire league is batting over .300, as the National League did in 1930?

Since 1940, fielding stats have continued to improve, but of course not at the pace set early in the century when there was so much room for improvement. By the decade of the 1970s, for example, the National League had pulled its fielding average up to .977. And its prorated season average for errors was down to 1,146. American League figures for the period would be about the same.

The improvement observable in fielding since the end of World War II is not, however, the kind easily measured by stats alone. The numbers haven't changed that much. It's more a matter of style. It involves daring, imagination, grace—but without sacrifice in precision. This change in style may have been what the late Gil Hodges, Brooklyn's superb first baseman, had in mind when he told Tom Meany in 1953, "Fielding has improved tremendously, even in the short time I have been in the majors." Ralph Kiner and other players of the time offered similar judgments.

It has always seemed to me that the mini-revolution in fielding had less to do with the popularity of bigger gloves than it did with the emergence in organized baseball of significant numbers of black and Hispanic players. Before five thousand professors of sociology drag me from my study to the nearest apple tree, let me shout in my defense, OK, OK, so it's an instance of acculturation. I won't argue. Still, I am reminded of Bill Veeck's comment that he can't offer a scrap of scientific evidence that black athletes run faster than whites, but every time he looks out on a playing field or track, that's what he sees.

In a 1971 article on Willie Mays in *Saturday Review*, Peter Schrag illustrates what I mean. He writes: "Mays was not merely a ballplayer who happened to be Negro; he was a black athlete. He ran black, swung black and caught black. He did not play the man's game but his own, and his every move disparaged the tight-assed honkies who did things by the book."

Later in the same piece, Schrag listens in as Willie instructs some young outfielders during spring training. "'You don't play it by the book,' he said. 'You play it opposite; you come up with the ball on the side you're going to throw. . . . Don't get directly in front of it . . . if you get in front of it you're playing it safe. You have to move everything, your arm, your legs, your body, keep it all moving; you're like a ballet dance out there; don't short-arm it, don't be afraid to let it go, and don't ever figure the ball's going to get by you.'"

This style, this élan—manifest not only in Mays but in Minnie Minoso, Roberto Clemente, Chico Carrasquel, Luis Aparicio, Vic Power, Curt Flood, Hank Aaron, and many others—cut off a lot of opposition runs. More important, it captured the imagination of the fans as fielding play never had before. And it seems to me that in the past thirty years, unconscious or otherwise, ballplayers of all races have adopted it—provided they had sufficient speed.

Something else that has greatly increased fan interest in fielding in the past quarter century is the Gold Glove Award. Stop a kid in the street today, quiz him about Gold Glove winners, and chances are he can tell you in a twinkling which National League catcher won in 1961 (L.A.'s Johnny Roseboro), just as in my youth a kid could probably tell you how many hits Chick Fullis had in 1933. (Two hundred, and what do you mean, you've never heard of Chick Fullis?) I guarantee you, though, that neither the kid of fifty years ago nor the Phillies' general manager could have told you how well Chick fielded that year. (It was .977, good for the era. And he led the league out-fielders in putouts.)

I've always felt that the advent of the Gold Glove Awards in 1957 must have been a wonderful morale booster for players who had been fielding their positions with distinction, but had little to show for it beyond an occasional compliment from a sportswriter. I asked Frank Malzone, the Boston Red Sox's great third baseman, win-ner of the first Gold Glove at that position. (In 1957, inci-

dentally, there was only one award for both leagues at
each position. Frank was undisputed best.) "Yes, I think
it did," Malzone said. "At least players began to talk more
about fielding in the clubhouse and other places. There's
no question that the Gold Glove became a goal that some
of them would shoot for and be disappointed if they didn't
win it."

But for all the apotheosis of the glove wizard in our
time, old habits of mind die hard. It's still a hitter's world.
Hall of Famer Brooks Robinson, who succeeded Malzone
as American League Gold Glove third baseman in 1960
and went on to win sixteen consecutive awards, told me:
"I played almost twenty-three years professionally and I
can never remember going in to a general manager to talk
about my contract and hearing him say, 'Brooks, how
many runs did you cut off?' Everything was based on what
you did offensively. Defense never even entered the picture."

Fortunately, Brooks swung a potent stick. So did Frank
Malzone. They couldn't have traded in those fielding tro-
phies for many groceries.

Happily, things have changed recently. Top-flight
fielders command respect now, even in the front office. It
is widely assumed that St. Louis shortstop Ozzie Smith
earns about one million dollars a year. I don't know anyone who was privy to Ozzie's contract negotiations, but
it's unlikely that his agent won him that kind of compensation on the strength of a .234 lifetime batting average.

Similarly, after helping the Chicago White Sox to a division title in 1983, light-hitting, but slick-fielding, second
baseman Julio Cruz was reported to have signed a long-
term contract at about $800,000 a season. The next thing
you know, they'll be naming a candy bar after some good-
field, no-hit superstar.

There's a story about Boston's hard-hitting third baseman Wade Boggs that charmingly illustrates fielding's
new image in the world. Boggs, who blistered American
League pitching for a .361 average in his first full season,
but who had occasional problems corralling ground balls,
told a reporter—perhaps a bit wistfully—"I'd like to get
credit for my fielding." Bless him.

We can also take heart from the recent election to the
Hall of Fame of premier glovemen like Luis Aparicio, Pee
Wee Reese, and Rick Ferrell. Not that great fielders have
failed to make Cooperstown in the past. It's just that their
cases were invariably strengthened by a .320 lifetime batting average or 400 home runs.

Yes, I can discourse for hours on the beauties, the subtleties, the virtues of good fielding. I can demonstrate to
my own intellectual satisfaction—and sometimes to that of
others—that in baseball, defense is the cornerstone of victory. But beneath the benign exterior I'm as bad as the
others. Let the thin end of a bat brush my palms and like
Doctor Jekyll I begin to twitch and snort. A change comes
over my person. I watch thick black hair sprout from the
back of my hand. To hell with making an unassisted triple
play, I growl through fangs. Just let me rap a two-run
double off the right-field wall.

It's human nature.

THREE

Glovemanship As Minor Art Form

"There are some fielders who make the impossible catch look ordinary and some the ordinary catch look impossible."

—JOE MCCARTHY

ONE OF THE CANONS OF OUR NATIONAL LIFE IS that the most difficult single act in all of sports is hitting a baseball. I think Ted Williams was first to say it. That's curious, too, because he is one of the few who ever made hitting look comparatively easy. The conventional evidence offered in confirmation of the doctrine is that major leaguers who succeed as little as 30 percent of the time are rewarded with multimillion-dollar contracts.

As owner of a largely unscarred Jimmie Foxx model Louisville Slugger, long buried under attic dust, I would be last to challenge baseball scripture on the difficulty of hitting. But let me suggest that catching a baseball is not easy either. It's just that no former superstar has come round to pontificating its complexities.

Many years ago, I read in one of the magazines of popular science that it would take a computer the size of Pharaoh Khufu's pyramid to duplicate the calculations performed in the brain of an outfielder while running down and catching a long fly ball. This was long before the microchip. Today, I suppose, it would call for a machine the size of a breadbox. I am still impressed.

Glib TV announcers and high-school baseball coaches notwithstanding, there is no such thing as an easy fly ball. Nor a routine grounder. Catching or scooping up a batted ball with consistency and throwing it with accuracy is tough at any level of play. For some fielders, just getting within range of the ball is a major accomplishment. Fans forget this. They get used to watching about seven hundred major leaguers perform these tasks with what looks like ease. We should all take another look at the movies from last summer's Lions Club picnic. Big-league ballplayers are, after all, the best of a population pool of possibly a hundred million men (if we include Canada and the Caribbean basin). When they are in the field they are setting themselves the highest standard of performance in sports. Acceptable levels of failure in fielding vary from position to position, of course, but on average 5 percent is close to intolerable. Anything above that will fetch you a ticket to the instructional league.

Stop and watch a kids' sandlot game. Better still, a high-school game. Often the hitting is impressive. Batters are selective: Many go with the pitch and a few can hit breaking stuff. Given the size of today's adolescents, you are likely to see a few balls hit clear out of the playing area. It's obvious that they get a lot of instruction. Pitchers are good, too. They are big and fast with fairly good control. Invariably, it's the fielding that's weak: overthrows galore, throws to the wrong base, fumbled grounders, an occasional dropped fly—and a lot of misjudged ones. It was the same when I was a kid, except that our hitting and pitching was lousy, too.

Why the disparity? Especially since in most instances our kids get good instruction in all aspects of the game. I can hear someone respond, "What teenager is interested in fielding? All they think about is hitting." I don't believe that. In my day, perhaps, but not today. We live in the age of the Gold Glove. It would be odd if a kid wearing a $140 glove didn't take pride in his fielding. What I suspect—and can't really prove—is that it has more to do with lack of physical maturity. Let me explain:

When a high-school third baseman bats, the pitching he faces is light-years removed from what Mike Schmidt sees in the National League. But when the high schooler is in the field and a batter taps a slow roller toward third, the kid confronts precisely the challenge that Schmidt does, plus the disadvantage of not playing on artificial surface or grass of major-league quality. Yes, I realize that the high-school base runner is not as fast as his National League counterpart, although he could be. What's sure is that the pickup and throw are equally difficult.

Obviously, ground balls in high school do not come off the bats with the same velocity that they do in the majors. On second thought, with those aluminum bats the kids use, how can we be sure? Anyway, grounders can take the same crazy bounces. And the distance between bases is still a full ninety feet. Fielding is a mighty leveler. A fly ball being deflected by the wind looks the same from below whether you're at Central Playground or Dodger Stadium.

In college baseball, the additional physical maturity seems to help narrow the disparity in performance among batting, baserunning, and fielding. I am guessing that it may be somewhere between the Class A and Class AAA minors that it disappears entirely. A disgruntled neighbor of mine, fan of a chronic loser, says that what really happens is that by the time players reach the majors their hitting has become as bad as their fielding.

Fielding is tough. And when properly executed, breathtaking to watch. To be sure, batting, pitching, and baserunning all have their high points of fluid motion, but they occur in a more restricted context than does fielding. Fielding invites interpretative execution. Willie Mays's analogy of the ballet dancer may not be farfetched. Maybe that's why poor fielding can be so painful to watch, quite apart from its consequences in the line score.

In his recent book on strategy, Earl Weaver observed, "Fielding is the most overlooked and may be the least understood talent in baseball." Why this should be so almost a century and a half after the game was created is a mystery. Tens of millions of fans watch baseball many times each summer. Many of them—men and women alike—have probably played the game at some level. Yet their ignorance of fielding is sometimes shocking.

An outfielder misjudges a fly ball and frantically reverses direction. With a desperate, last-second lunge or dive he makes the catch. The crowd cheers wildly. A second outfielder is off at the crack of the bat (or earlier), races back eighty feet, turns, and stands, waiting for the ball to come down. The fans yawn and order another beer. Maybe I'm too harsh. It's possible they are expressing relief in the first instance.

I am reminded of a play I watched on television during the 1958 World Series. I can't recall the game or the inning, only that it was played in Milwaukee. The Yankees were at bat with a man on first; the batter hit a hard hopper toward the gap on the right side, just out of reach of Milwaukee first baseman Frank Torre, who was holding the runner. But second baseman Red Schoendienst ran it down at the edge of the grass and, with one smooth, continuous motion, turned 360 degrees and cut down the lead runner at second with a perfect throw. To my astonishment, the home crowd gave no more acknowledgment than if Schoendienst had taken a pop fly behind the pitcher's mound. I have tried to tell myself since that Red simply had them spoiled with his superb style of play. Anyway, I like to believe that fans today are more sophisticated.

Baseball is intensely remembered, Roger Angell says, because only baseball is so intensely watched. But maybe we still fall short of the intensity necessary to grasp fully what happens on some of the finest fielding plays. To begin with, baseball play is actually spread out. There is never the bunching together that characterizes football and basketball.

Years ago, one of the baseball announcers—maybe it was Red Barber—recommended that fans at the park try taking their eyes off the flight of the ball momentarily to watch the fielders move and position themselves on different plays. It's not easy to take your eye off the ball. We are all conditioned to locking on it to the exclusion of other action. Think how much more appreciation we have for body movement and form when watching such events as figure skating, platform diving, even boxing, where there is no ball or puck to monopolize our attention. And what would most of us know about the subtleties of interior line play if TV's instant replay did not isolate and preserve the action for us?

It's likely that instant replay on television is also doing

its share to educate fans about fielding. A slow-motion replay of Brooks Robinson or Graig Nettles levitating as he cuts off a sure extra-base hit down the left-field line lets us review in detail the extraordinary alertness and agility of these men. On tape we see how gracefully a big man like Dave Concepcion leaps over the hard-sliding base runner while making a perfect relay to first on a double play that happens so fast it is difficult for the imagination to reconstruct it.

In fact, videotape may have helped lay to rest forever the mild complaint registered by Charlie Gehringer, Detroit's great second baseman of the 1920s and 1930s, in an interview with Donald Honig. "Hitting is the thing that people remember most vividly," Charlie said. "You can make the greatest fielding play in the world, and they probably won't remember it the next day. Particularly in the infield." Today, not only does the fan see the play on the field, but if it's an exciting one, it is replayed from videotape on the big scoreboards, repeated on the late-night news when the fan gets home, and, if it affected the outcome of an important game, it may be rerun on special occasions for years. How many times have you seen replays of Billy Martin's catch of Jackie Robinson's infield pop-up in the 1952 World Series? I don't care if they rerun it five hundred times. It reminds me of how a game or a series can hang on a heads-up fielding play.

I think what fans most often fail to appreciate is the coordinated movements of the whole team in the field. Every fielder has an assignment on every play. How often do you check to see if the pitcher backed up third on a double down the right-field line? Sure, you're too busy watching the ball. So am I. But it's imperative that the pitcher and everyone else carry out his assignment to guard against the possibility of that runner getting beyond second. When you stop to think about it, only in the field do baseball players function as a team. Batting is essentially a one-man show, even with the bases loaded.

Normally I am not inclined to violence. The exception is when I find myself in the company of a baseball illiterate. Often at cocktail parties I will overhear some moonraker whine, "I can't stand baseball. Nothing ever happens between home runs. Just nine guys standing around looking at each other." Faster than you can say Van Lingle Mungo I am in a mood to seize the villain by the collar and dash his vacuous face in the onion dip. Fortunately, it has never quite come to that. When the offender is a woman I have considered asking if she could possibly be the same Imogene Barnswallow who was in my father's class in high school. But I haven't yet sunk to such cruelty.

Nine guys standing around indeed. No team game ever devised demands of its players such intense and refined coordination, such split-second timing, such collective concentration on every play. Fielders not only have to realign themselves for each batter, they must make subtle adjustments for each pitch. As often as 150 times a game each man on the field must be up on his toes, leaning, or even in motion before the ball is hit. He must know exactly what he will do if the ball should be hit to him or if it should be hit to any one of eight others.

Take a hit into the gap in right center with a man on first. It's a race between man and ball, one of the most exciting plays in any sport. A run is at stake, possibly the winning run. The right fielder and center fielder converge on the ball, one to back up the man who can best make the play. The second baseman moves into short right center to relay the throw. The shortstop must trail the second baseman to guard against a poor throw from the outfield and then be prepared to cover second. The first baseman acts as cutoff man and the third baseman covers third. The left fielder backs up third base and the pitcher backs up the plate. The catcher, of course, must be ready to take the relay and tag the runner trying to score.

In most cases, if the runner is to be kept from scoring, the relay must be perfect. Not just pretty good, but perfect. This play often results in a close decision at the plate. With the very best team play in the field, you come down to a matter of inches. What more can you ask in the way of action?

The importance of teamwork and execution was perfectly illustrated during the 1946 World Series between the Boston Red Sox and the St. Louis Cardinals. In the eighth inning of game seven, with the score tied at three and the Cardinals' Enos "Country" Slaughter on first with two out, Harry Walker hit what appeared to be a long single to left center. On this kind of hit the speedy Slaughter would be expected to advance to third with no difficulty. But the hard-driving Country had no intention of stopping at third. The series was on the line.

Taking the throw from the outfield, shortstop Johnny Pesky, the Red Sox's relay man, held the ball for a split second before going to the plate. Perhaps he assumed that Slaughter had held up at third. When he did throw, Slaughter beat it for what proved to be the series-winning run. For years, Pesky bore the wrath of the multitude for the late throw. It was a bum rap. Pesky might have been the only man on the field who had his back to the play. Anyone could have called to him to throw home. We have to assume that no one did. Nine men were involved in the play. In my book they share the responsibility for Slaughter's run equally.

At different times both Yogi Berra and Branch Rickey have counseled us that it is best for a batter not to think.

As Rickey put it, "A full mind is an empty bat." Not so for the man wearing a glove. He must be thinking all the time. As long as the ball is in play, there is something going on that could involve him directly and affect the welfare of the team. He must ponder this *before the ball is hit* and be in the most advantageous position to help.

In the old days, a fielder was expected to keep his own book on every hitter in the league and keep it up to date in his head. It was customary for teams to go over the opposing lineup in a pregame meeting, and a manager or catcher might reposition fielders occasionally depending on the situation. But, ultimately, each fielder was responsible for positioning himself according to the known strengths of the batter. In recent years, the use of exhaustive pitching charts, situation charts, and, in some cases, computers may have taken the romance out of positioning, but a fan who is not aware of how fielders realign themselves for each batter is missing an important part of the game.

I have a hunch that many popular misconceptions about fielding stem in part from the bombast of influential figures like Rogers Hornsby, who said more than fifty years ago that you can shake great fielders out of the trees but that hitters will always be hard to come by. If that had in fact been the situation in Hornsby's day—and it comes closer to truth today—a succession of Brooklyn managers might have spent most of their daylight hours shaking trees. Ironically, when Hornsby was managing, .340 hitters were plentiful and second basemen were booting fifty chances a season. Maybe the notoriously arrogant Rajah, who batted over .400 three times in four years, did not regard anything under .390 as real hitting.

I discount Hornsby's hyperbole about the availability of great gloves. But an observation on fielding from another batting wizard, Ted Williams, is worth some thought. "There's a saying that you can't make a hitter," Ted commented once, "but I think you can improve a hitter. More than you can improve a fielder." It surprised me when I first read it. Never an industrious gloveman himself, Williams is nevertheless one of the most profound students of the game—in all its aspects. If he has suggestions about how the grass should be cut around the third-base coaching box, I treat it as though it were advice from E. F. Hutton.

For a long time, Williams's view on the difficulty of improving a fielder puzzled me. There had been, after all, some widely publicized and heartwarming cases of self-improvement—Hank Greenberg, Lou Gehrig, Harmon Killebrew, Eddie Mathews. But maybe what these men learned was how to position their feet, where to throw the ball—that sort of thing. I finally decided that what Ted meant was that the instinct for catching the ball and throwing it straight is God-given and there's not much that a coach can do once the genes have been distributed. If that is so, it helps to explain some ancient attitudes about defensive skills.

In reading the memoirs of former ballplayers, I used to be struck by the testimony of the old-timers that little was done to help them make the grade in the big leagues. It was not always expected of a rookie that he would begin hitting .300 the day he stepped off the train from Altoona. He might even receive a grudging batting tip from his manager or the rare compassionate veteran. But it appeared to be an article of faith that he was already a major-league fielder, that the skill had come with his mother's milk. Why else would he have chosen a career in baseball?

To confirm my impression of the traditional treatment

of rookies in the old days, I asked Harlond Clift, who broke in with the St. Louis Browns in 1934 and was for many years a power-hitting third baseman and a good fielder. Harlond was blunt: "In all my professional career of hitting, fielding, running and thinking, no one offered to teach me a thing," he said. "I had to do it all on my own." There may have been just a bit of mischief in my choice of witness. Clift's first big-league manager was Rogers Hornsby.

Since clubs back in those days had a considerable investment riding on the success or failure of young players—just as they do now—I can only conclude that there was a widespread conviction that if you didn't have it from the cradle, you weren't going to get it. It would have brought a smile to Darwin's lips.

Today, of course, the attitude toward training seems more enlightened. Maybe the clubs are just hedging their bets, but they do maintain extensive instructional staffs, including not only batting and pitching instructors, but also men to teach fielding, baserunning, and catching. Bill Heywood, the Seattle Mariners' assistant director of player development for instruction, told me that his club retains a staff of roving instructors in fielding to work with their minor-league players at each level. "We're exposing kids to things they might not think of until two or three years down the road. The more you expose them, hopefully, the quicker they'll catch on. You take a young man who has trouble trying to make the double play. Good instruction can help him get his footwork together, get his hands in position."

I asked Heywood about the theory that essential fielding skill is innate. "I won't argue with that," he said. "I tell our kids every day that somebody greater than I gave them that ability. Now it's up to them to learn to use that ability to its potential."

The Cardinals' great Marty Marion, known universally in the 1940s as "Mr. Shortstop," volunteered a similar view without my even asking the question. "To me fielding is a kind of gift," Marty said. "You really can't teach a guy to field a ball. I'm sure that most fielders in the major leagues were never taught to field. They can improve a little bit, yes. But you either have it or you don't."

Williams, Heywood, and Marion make me feel better. I have stopped berating myself for booting that perfect double-play ball with the bases loaded back in high school. And, of course, I don't blame my coach. Now I denounce my parents.

It's worth noting that no one has ever suggested that practice won't help even the most gifted fielder sharpen his skills. Earl Weaver reports that in spring training, players like Brooks Robinson and Mark Belanger would take a hundred practice ground balls a day. As you can see, the very best don't just relax and let the genes take over. They make doubly sure.

Since the subject of practice has come up, let me digress briefly to put in a word for the noble game of stickball as a nurturer of the soft hands so prized by fielders. Classically, stickball is played on a congested city street with a simple rubber ball and a broomstick for a bat. A manhole cover makes a serviceable, if somewhat overlarge, home plate, and fielders must accept the risk of dodging among parked cars and vaulting fire hydrants to make the big play.

Now, I'll admit that as a relatively privileged youth, living far from the inner city, I have never experienced stickball in its purest form. Usually, our games were played in spacious schoolyards on carefully measured diamonds set within painted foul lines. At worst we might repair to a nearby development tract, where streets had been platted and paved but where, owing to the Depression, neither houses nor cars were yet in evidence.

In those days—and perhaps still—stickball called for a Spalding pink rubber ball of prodigal liveliness, known in the youthful argot of the period as a "spaldeen." It was said of a brand-new and genuine spaldeen that if dropped from eye level it should rebound to half your height. Novelist Alan Furst tells me that in his neighborhood on New York's Upper West Side, where it appears kids were abnormally distrustful of marketing claims, it was customary to drop a new spaldeen from an eight-story building to see if it would bounce back four. He's not sure how many balls passed the test.

Imagine if you can what happened to a spaldeen when hit by a whiplike broomstick in the hands of some urchin with the bat speed of a Jim Rice. Even in the then pollution-free skies over the borough of Queens, fly balls customarily disappeared from view on their five-hundred-foot suborbital flights. Reentry was often a nightmare for outfielders. Misshapen from the force of the blow, the ball might resemble two pullet eggs flying in tandem. Catching a fly, I can assure you, called for heroic concentration and the most patient hands you've ever seen.

Infielders had it worse. All but the most foolhardy played back about 120 feet. Running the extra distance to cover a base was preferable to risking disembowelment by a line drive. Ordinary grounders looked like chalk streaks on the asphalt school ground. Hard-hit ones were invisible. Assists, need I say, were rare. If you could come up with just one in a game, you knew you had a real pair of hands.

Mercifully, one swinging strike was out in stickball. Otherwise, some of the teams I faced back in 1936 would still be batting.

Not content with my own assessment, I conferred with veteran stickballer Frank Malzone, who later with the Red Sox parlayed his dexterity into several Gold Gloves. Now, I won't claim that Frank was dazzled by my thesis, but in his always gentlemanly fashion he allowed as how any game played with a lively rubber ball was probably good for hand-eye coordination. In fact, he put in a plug for a stickball spin-off called punchball, in which a balled fist or opened palm was substituted for a broom or mop handle. Punchball seems to have risen to prominence during the Depression, when some mothers put a moratorium on incursions into the kitchen closet. For obvious reasons, Frank feels that punchball probably afforded the playground infielder somewhat more reasonable practice than did stickball in corralling a lively ball.

Since leaving the country of stickball many years ago, I have watched kids in various places playing catch and other games with rubber balls and tennis balls. And I'll bet that if you checked with Julio Cruz, Lou Whitaker, Dickie Thon, and a lot of these magicians with the glove, you would find that they spent long hours as kids trying to get their hands around a bouncing rubber ball. I think that my theory has merit and I was pleased to learn recently that the Milwaukee Brewers organization starts out its young catchers snagging a tennis ball, with and without a mitt. I may even propose to the president of one of the rookie leagues that he schedule stickball games in the afternoon as a prelude to the regular baseball game at night.

It's curious the way we impose an aesthetic dimension in our judgment of fielders. What I mean is that we judge a fielder not only on whether he gets the runner out, but also on how he looks while he's doing it. Two second basemen throw out runners on nearly identical ground balls hit to the right of the bag. One is very smooth in his movements; he makes the play look easy. The other also gets the runner, but he scrambles for the ball ("stands on his head," as they say). We judge the first as the better fielder.

Batting, baserunning, and pitching, on the other hand, are largely bottom-line skills. If the man gets the job done, we don't much care how he does it. Remember George Shuba, a utility outfielder with Brooklyn's Boys of Summer? It was said that George had the most perfect swing in baseball. But that swing netted him a .259 lifetime batting average. By contrast, Lou Gehrig often looked like a rusty gate in a high wind as he turned baseballs to jelly. Take your pick. Then there was the Cardinals' Joe Medwick, who was known to tomahawk pitches that were over his head—for home runs. If a batter has a picture swing—Charlie Gehringer, Fred Lynn, Steve Garvey—we don't hold it against him, just so long as he has that picture batting average to go with it.

In fielding we view grace and ease as part of getting the job done. Our greatest admiration has been reserved for the men whose movements were the most fluid—Larry Lajoie, George Sisler, Edd Roush, Charlie Gehringer, Joe DiMaggio, Roberto Clemente, Ozzie Smith. Can anyone who ever saw him play forget DiMaggio's effortless stride as he was in the process of robbing someone of a triple?

But is the standard fair? Now that I think of it, I am hard pressed to name you a truly graceful player who was not also a great fielder. I have never heard of one who charmed the crowd with his movements while he was dropping fly balls. On the other side of the ledger there are fielders who have done an excellent job of retiring batters while not looking exactly stylish doing it. Frankie

Frisch often looked like he was wrestling with ground balls, but very few ever got past him. Eddie Stanky was somewhat the same. And probably their reputations in the field suffered.

Perhaps the most puzzling victim of the double standard we impose is Pete Rose. Pete has won a couple of Gold Gloves, it is true, but he is not thought of by the fans as an outstanding fielder and probably never will be. Yet his record is remarkable.

Rose has held down five different positions as a regular and has won fielding titles in four of them. In eight full seasons in the outfield for Cincinnati—a total of 1,220 games—he made just twenty errors. In the same period he made ninety-seven assists. And no one has ever accused Pete of not trying for every ball hit in his direction. As I write this he still holds the all-time record for fielding average by an outfielder.

Researcher Bill Deane, an authority on fielding stats, has made a special study of Rose's performance. He writes, "Considering the three factors of versatility, durability and effectiveness, Pete Rose is the best defensive player in baseball history." Bill will get no argument from me. After almost a quarter of a century of watching Rose play—admittedly in probably fewer than a hundred games—I can recall seeing him make only one error, and that was on a throw to try to cut off the go-ahead run in a World Series game.

Clearly, when judging fielders we place a high premium on form. Perhaps our senses force us to it.

After years of studying this demanding, frustrating, incomparably rewarding game of baseball, I am convinced that the finest fielders mature later and fade earlier than do either great hitters or outstanding pitchers. I'm talking now about their peak of skills, before they lose that precious half step or some elasticity in the arm. The period would doubtless vary from position to position, briefer for a shortstop or center fielder, longer for a first baseman. And it does not follow that the player is ready for the glue factory when that perfection of execution is past. I am not aware of a department of sports medicine that has yet made a study of the phenomenon, but I am not going to be surprised when evidence of the shooting-star character of top defensive skills is scientifically documented.

Take a look at what the hitters and pitchers can do when they start to gray around the temples. At thirty-nine, Ted Williams combed American League pitching for a .388 average. At the same age, Hank Aaron belted forty home runs. At forty-two, Stan Musial had been whittled down to a mere .330 by National League pitchers, and his contemporary, Warren Spahn, barely had the strength to win twenty-three games. Luke Appling still had enough mustard left in his swing at seventy-five to loft a pitch into the stands of RFK Stadium in Washington, D.C., but he would be first to tell you that it's been many decades since he was able to go deep in the hole for a hard grounder.

Enough of this discussion. It makes me nervous and depressed. I have an impulse to throw a dust cover on the typewriter and rush to the ball park while Alan Trammell, Dale Murphy, and Ryne Sandberg are still under thirty. I fear missing even one golden moment of glove magic. Hitters? I would not go so far as to say that when you've seen one, you've seen them all, but there is a numbing sameness about home runs.

In my mind's eye I see the tying run on second, two out in the ninth. The batter rifles a hit to right field. The lithe young right fielder charges the ball, scoops, and with a grand sweeping motion looses a low throw to the plate. The throw is so low, in fact, that the cutoff man has to duck slightly to keep from being hit. The ball comes on one long hop to the catcher waiting on the line. The catcher drops to his knees, blocking the plate. A tangle of bodies. Out. Beautiful.

Bases loaded, tying run on third, one out. The batter hits a hard smash to the right of second. The wiry little second baseman, in motion before the crack of the bat, reaches across his body to spear the grounder just as it's about to escape into center field. Without straightening, he flips a waist-high throw over the bag. The rangy short-stop takes the throw in full stride, leaps lightly over the sliding base runner, twists his upper body to the right, and at the height of his leap fires the ball to the first base-man, whose gloved hand is stretched toward second as far as his tall frame will permit. Double play. Elapsed time: under four seconds. Magnificent. In fact, I don't believe you will see it topped at Lincoln Center.

FOUR
Calluses to Peachbaskets

*"I don't care how big they make the gloves, you
still have to catch the ball."*
      —ETHAN ALLEN
            Former major league outfielder
            and Yale baseball coach

THE FIRST BASEBALL GLOVE I EVER OWNED WAS
a flat piece of red-dyed horsehide, slightly larger than a
motorman's gauntlet. I doubt that it cost more than two
dollars when my father bought it for me at a Davega store
on New York's West Thirty-fourth Street as a kind of celebration present after we had watched the Giants crush
one of their hated rivals of the period, probably the Cubs
or the Cardinals. I must have been about ten or eleven
and the new mitt made me feel as formidable as Mel Ott.
      As I remember the glove it had stubby fingers and a

single loop of rawhide connecting the index finger and the thumb. It was essentially a single layer of horsehide, undressed surface to the inside. Except for the heel, where it was not much needed, the glove had little padding. In fact, the padding was detachable, just some kapok or matted wool sewn into cloth tubes. No pocket. The tradition was that you created your own pocket by pounding the palm of the glove with your fist or a ball. After months of pounding, the knuckles of my right hand were beautifully callused. The glove was as flat as the day I got it.

I was reminded of this when my sons were old enough to have their first fielder's gloves. The preformed pockets were deep enough to conceal a grapefruit. Today, my grandson's glove looks like the Rose Bowl modeled in blond leather.

Despite deficiencies in the design, the little red glove helped me develop a feel for the ball. In fact, the feel sometimes lasted until Thanksgiving. It was about then that the redness and swelling in my palm had gone down enough so that I could clench the fingers of my left hand. Anyway, unless protective amnesia is working overtime, I remember dropping few throws and no fly balls.

By the time I reached high school I had advanced to a state-of-the-art glove: double layer of soft leather, generous padding, preformed pocket, leather strip between thumb and first finger, and laces joining a couple of the other fingers. Beautiful. It was a Wally Berger model. That's akin to having a Mark Belanger bat. The old Boston Braves' slugger was never mistaken for Terry Moore when covering center field. But Wally was "adequate," as we used to say, and I can tell you for sure that he was wearing a fine glove.

I find that the subject of baseball gloves and their effect on the game can spark more controversy than a Jim Watt press conference. It's been going on since the 1880s, when glove manufacturer George Wright warned that these instruments of the devil might make hitters an endangered species. George was a hitter first, an entrepreneur second. Of course, he raised this alarm right after the St. Louis Browns' Tip O'Neill finished the 1887 season at .435. I guess George was just the worrying type.

In 1894, Boston's Hugh Duffy hit .438 and had a slugging percentage of .679. In Philadelphia that season, five regulars batted a collective .401 and the entire team weighed in with .349. As a matter of fact, the twelve-team National League hit .309 for the year.

How did the rules committee react to this onslaught? In the following year they restricted the size and weight of the gloves. Maybe they thought they could get Duffy up to about .475. In fact, the poor fellow tailed off to an anemic .352. But five other guys batted over .390.

The 1920 season saw the single greatest revolution in glove design with the appearance of the Bill Doak model. It had a preformed pocket and reinforced webbing. Here was a direct threat to a hitter's livelihood. What to do? Well, over the next five years, Hornsby, Cobb, Sisler, and Harry Heilmann rolled up a total of seven .400-plus seasons with Babe Ruth and Tris Speaker just a step behind them. For the whole decade of the twenties, the two leagues batted a reassuring .287 in the face of the Bill Doak menace. It does make you wonder.

I ask a famous, glue-fingered major leaguer why the fielding is better today than it was in the past and he tells me it's all because of the big gloves. Then he adds that he has always used a small glove because it improved his fielding.

Or I turn on the TV just in time to watch some ham-handed slugger let a perfect throw drop from the pocket of his custom-made, four-hundred-dollar first baseman's mitt.

What's the poor fan to believe?

For a starter I'll believe what Red Barber told me: "You always come down to the abilities of the individual." In fact, I have no doubt that if you put Dickie Thon, Mark Belanger, and Luis Aparicio in Honus Wagner's old glove, you would still have three Gold Glove shortstops. Put Honus in Willie Aikens's first baseman's mitt—or no mitt at all—and you would have an all-time shortstop.

There's one point on which everyone seems agreed. Gloves were first introduced as protection for the hands rather than to enhance fielding, though logically it would seem to come to the same thing. As a matter of fact, a few old-timers continued to field bare-handed well into the 1890s, stoically nursing their bone bruises out of a conviction that the newfangled leather contraption was actually an encumbrance. And when a guy could go get the ball as well as Cincinnati's Bid McPhee, who was going to talk him into wearing a glove?

The early history of baseball gloves is still shrouded in mystery. No one knows for sure who first hollered uncle and wrapped his throbbing hand in buckskin so that he could continue play.

A widely circulated story has Cincinnati Red Stocking catcher Doug Allison the first to appear on a field wearing a glove. Another version says that it was Nat Hicks, who caught for the New York Mutuals. The fact that they were both catchers adds a note of credibility. Still, it's hard to believe that no one before the 1870s considered the expedient of covering his hands to take some of the sting out of a thrown or batted ball. I suppose we'll never know.

The earliest documented use of a glove by a professional

ballplayer was by St. Louis outfielder Charlie Waitt (you may see his name misspelled at times) in 1875. The principal source for this is Al Spalding's autobiographical *America's National Game*, first published in 1911. Spalding, the consummate entrepreneur and promoter of his own interests, is not always viewed as a reliable conduit of baseball lore. Among other things he has been charged with engineering the Abner Doubleday legend.

At all events, Spalding writes that one day in 1875 Waitt (he spells it Waite) appeared on the field at Boston wearing an ordinary street-dress leather glove on his left hand. It was flesh colored, presumably to avoid detection from the stands. Waitt, Spalding says, had cut a section from the back of the glove to allow for ventilation. On the strength of evidence from sources other than Spalding, there is reason to believe that on this occasion or others, Charlie actually wore two gloves and cut the fingers from the one on his throwing hand.

According to Spalding, fans around the league ridiculed Waitt without mercy for what looked like a sissy act. The Boston pitching star guessed that the hostile fan reaction may have discouraged other players from trying gloves. Despite the risk to reputation, Spalding goes on to report, he followed Waitt's lead when he shifted from pitcher to first base in 1877. He decided that he had had enough of swollen palms and jammed fingers. So that the fans would not mistake his intention, Spalding showed up at first base wearing a padded glove of dark leather rather than flesh color. This time there were no catcalls from the stands. Implicit in Spalding's story is that once the great man himself had lent approval to the new equipment, no barrier to its use was conceivable.

It is worth noting that in 1876, the year after Charlie Waitt had braved the derision of the fans, Spalding and his brother established a sporting-goods company that in time was to dominate the business of producing baseball equipment. What could be more appropriate than that the legendary Al should be first to win over the fans to the use of baseball gloves. Ring those cash registers.

There is also a story that Arthur Irwin, a highly respected shortstop for a number of National League teams in the 1880s and 1890s, was the first to create a serviceable padded fielder's glove. That was in 1882. Understandably, Irwin's claim was strongly promoted by the Draper-Maynard Company of Plymouth, New Hampshire, which first marketed the Irwin glove. Since it can be established that the Spaldings were advertising their gloves for sale as early as 1878, what Irwin came up with could have been a new design. The best guess is that it was the earliest glove with padded fingers, since Draper-Maynard concurrently marketed a fingerless, thumbless glove for "the throwing hand." Irwin, incidentally, may have been the first Canadian-born player to make the big leagues.

It doesn't take a genius to surmise that it was the catchers of the 1870s and 1880s who had the most pressing concerns about stinging palms and broken fingers. In any case, there have probably been more claimants to the invention of the catcher's mitt than there used to be G.A.R. vets who swore they had fought at Gettysburg. But since necessity, especially painful necessity, is the mother of you-know-what, it could be that all claims about the origin of the catcher's mitt are equally true.

An old fellow named Joe Gunson, who got into a couple of hundred big-league games in the 1880s, testified to having jerry-built the first catcher's mitt when he was playing in the Western League in 1888. According to Gunson, the mitt was fashioned from canvas, sheepskin, and buckskin, and was stiffened with the wire handle from a paint can.

Joe made no attempt to conceal the design, and he hints—
without rancor—that Harry Decker, widely credited with
having designed the first thickly padded catcher's glove,
borrowed the idea and took it to the Reach Company,
where they produced the famous "Decker patent" glove.

Decker's mitt appeared in 1891. But there is a steel en-
graving of Buck Ewing, done in the mid-1880s, which
shows the famous New York Giant catcher wearing a sizable padded glove on his left hand and a fingerless glove
on his throwing hand. In all probability what Harry
Decker did was to consolidate and refine a number of ideas
for catchers' gloves that were already in circulation.

As late as 1932, an old man named Paul Buckley, who
claimed to have caught for both the legendary Chicago
White Stockings and the equally storied St. Louis
Browns, told *The Seattle Post-Intelligencer* that in 1889,
tired of suffering broken fingers several times a season, he
invented and patented the first catcher's mitt and
promptly sold the rights to Spalding Brothers for ten
thousand dollars. Unfortunately, there is no record of
Buckley's having played with any major-league team. Gettysburg again?

It appears likely that by the mid-1890s, the use of
gloves in professional baseball was just about universal.
In any case, the rules committee felt moved in 1895 to
limit the size of gloves officially. A catcher or first baseman, they ruled, was free to use a glove of any size. All
other players were restricted to a glove of ten ounces or
lighter, and one no more than fourteen inches in circumference, measured around the palm.

A handful of veteran ballplayers served out their days
bare-handed, notably Cincinnati second baseman Bid
McPhee and another second baseman, Fred Dunlap, who
played for Cleveland and several other teams. These men

were well-established professionals, stars actually. It's not likely that theirs was an act of bravado. They must have been convinced that they could field better without gloves. At the same time there lingered in baseball a grudging acknowledgment that it took a real man to play the old-fashioned way. Why else would an intelligent, well-educated player like Fred Tenney, the superlative first baseman for the perennial champion Boston Bean-eaters (they were really called that), toss aside his mitt during fielding practice and demonstrate to the crowd that he could take the hottest throws from his infielders bare-handed?

I am guessing that after the use of gloves was thoroughly established early in this century there must have been a fair amount of tinkering and fiddling with them by the players to satisfy individual needs. It's the American way. Unfortunately, there's scant record of such modifications aside from the curious custom of cutting the palm out of a fielder's glove, which a surprising number of players did in the years before World War I. They must have been nostalgic for the feel of the ball. But more about this bare-hand business later.

The most thoroughly documented case of an idea for glove design to come directly from a player was that of Cardinals pitcher "Spittin' Bill" Doak. In 1919, Doak went to the Rawlings Company, which was right in St. Louis, with some suggestions for improving the effectiveness of the fielder's glove. Doak's glove featured a multithonged web, laced into the thumb and index finger, and a pre-formed, prelubricated pocket. In effect, the glove did not have to be broken in. By 1920, Rawlings was mass marketing the Bill Doak model and it revolutionized the future design of all gloves, including first baseman's mitts and catcher's mitts. Remarkably, the Doak glove remained in regular production into the 1950s. From the very beginning, incidentally, the Bill Doak was available in both short-fingered and long-fingered versions.

All the while that gloves were being invented and improved, fielding kept getting better. How much this steady advance in skill could be directly attributed to gloves is hard to say. Some, certainly, but remember that bare-handed stalwarts like McPhee and Dunlap were still pretty slick when measured against their gloved contemporaries. I can tell you for sure that by the 1930s and 1940s, baseball gloves had reached such a high level of quality that no player of that era would have dared to suggest that his glove was to blame for his poor fielding. He would have been laughed off the field.

Since memory can be tricky in such matters, I thought I had better verify my recollection of those days with Marty "Slats" Marion, who arrived in St. Louis in 1940. "Oh, my, yes, we had good gloves," Marty told me. "They weren't as large as they are now, but they were nice-sized gloves. I have no complaints about the gloves that I used."

Marion also called to my attention that back in the thirties and forties, any big-league player could have had a larger glove if he wanted one. "Rawlings would have made you one for the asking," he said. And, in fact, Rawlings did make a big one for Cardinals pitcher Morton Cooper in 1942. No, "Big Mort" was not interested in improving his already excellent fielding. (He was a converted catcher, by the way.) He wanted the oversized glove to conceal his pitching grip from the inquiring eyes of opposing coaches.

Considering the paranoia about gloves among the disciples of ash, it's remarkable that there were no major revisions in the rules governing gloves between 1895 and 1950. In 1931, the committee did specify that all gloves must be made of leather and that the pitcher's should be uniform in color. I don't know what gave rise to that one. Possibly the committee had received advance word that the plastics industry was about to envelop the world with their products. Plastic gloves may well prevail in the future. The way they keep expanding the majors, there can't be enough cows in the world to supply the players with leather gloves.

The most significant development in gloves between the world wars was a modest elaboration in the webbing (an outgrowth of the Bill Doak model). Though it affected all gloves, it may have had the most significance for the design of first baseman's mitts and catcher's mitts. As a matter of fact, it was Detroit first baseman Hank Greenberg, a hardworking, self-improvement type, who got himself involved in a major controversy in the 1930s over the webbing of a mitt that he had designed himself.

I am not sure how large Greenberg's mitt was, though my impression is that it was noticeably bigger than the conventional one of the day, but quite within the rules, of course, since there was no restriction on size. It was the webbing—described by some writers as a "fish net"—that caused the ruckus. I guess that once a throw from shortstop got lodged in Hank's glove, not even Marv Throneberry could have shaken it out.

After a superheated logomachy generated by opposing American League managers, Commissioner Kenesaw Mountain Landis ruled that Greenberg's creation was suitable only for the Smithsonian and that the big first baseman would have to make do with an assembly-line model. Reacting to the Donnybrook, the rules committee in 1939 laid down that from that time on, first baseman's mitts could measure not more than twelve inches from top to bottom, nor more than eight inches across the palm. Most important, the webbing was limited to four inches from thumb to palm with no hanky-panky about its rigidity. No more fish nets.

Funny thing about the Hank Greenberg flap is that the very next year, Rawlings introduced the trapper-style mitt, which had an extra "finger" between the thumb and palm and may have had about the same effect as Hank's glove—closing the glove around the ball. But it was not a net and presumably fell within the rules.

The trapper concept remained popular among first basemen for almost a decade. Then, unaccountably, there was another dustup, and in 1949 the rules committee outlawed the design. The ink was scarcely dry on the ukase when the committee reversed itself. Clearly, it was long past time to sit down and have a hard look at the rules governing gloves, and in 1950 the committee did just that. They threw out the old restrictions on the weight of gloves, which wasn't being adhered to anyway, and concentrated on limiting glove size, except for catcher's mitts. The mistake they made was in not specifying how and by whom the gloves were to be measured.

The new rules worked pretty well for about ten years. Then, Baltimore manager Paul Richards, who had knuckleballer Hoyt Wilhelm on his pitching staff, ran out of patience as his catchers threatened to break Ernie Lombardi's record for passed balls. The Waxahachie Wizard commissioned the Wilson Company to make him the biggest catcher's mitt you have ever seen. It was only slightly smaller than a trash-can lid and must have had a webbing about a foot wide. It was also hinged. Wilhelm and catcher Clint Courtney put it to the test in May 1960.

Oh, it worked all right. In fact, it worked fine; that was the trouble. Opposing teams howled in protest. If they had to face Wilhelm's maddening butterfly pitches, they at least wanted the compensation of passed balls and wild pitches. Back to the drawing board for the rules committee. They shaved catcher's mitts down to thirty-eight inches in circumference (still pretty big, actually) and fifteen and a half inches from top to bottom. Richards says the explanation the committee offered him was that the big glove was causing a distraction on telecasts of the games. Top that if you can.

By the early 1970s it was apparent to the least observant that fielder's gloves were rapidly approaching the size of a kiddy pool. Little Leaguers were walking around with their left shoulders permanently lowered from trying to bear the weight. It was typically American. As one equipment manufacturer explained it, "If a big glove is good, then the players think that an even bigger glove is better. We couldn't keep within the rule and not face the loss of business to the bigger glove."

The 1950 rule on fielder's gloves had been specific enough on size. Where it failed was in setting ground rules for how they were to be measured. In the 1960s, manufacturers must have been putting the tape to the gloves when they were bent double. In 1972, at the direction of Commissioner Bowie Kuhn, the rules committee reworded Rule 1.14 so that even a platoon of personal-injury lawyers would be hard pressed to find a loophole. The committee went so far as to append a drawing to the rule, spelling out how each finger of the glove was to be measured. So far, this version of the rule is holding up and today's players seem well able to gather in the ball with a fielder's glove that's a mere twelve inches long and seven and three quarters inches wide.

Under gentle persuasion from Commissioner Kuhn, a generation of professional ballplayers appears convinced that they can get the job done with reasonably sized, even small, gloves. Not so amateurs, especially kids. A lot of youngsters today are haunted by the notion that the glove does the fielding, not the guy who's wearing it. Some of this thinking may reflect fallout from manufacturers' claims or, at least, implied claims. Since kids today apparently worry more about their fielding than they did when I was young, they won't consider anything less than the most monstrous glove that can be smuggled across the border. It's the same logic that moves a Little Leaguer to crave a forty-eight-ounce bat.

In a sense the glovemaker has been hoist with his own petard. A representative of one of the big houses told me, "Sure we make small gloves. Infielders' gloves are not the same as outfielders' gloves. In fact we make them to meet the special needs of every position. But that's pretty much for pros and colleges. It's hard to sell dealers a small glove for the same price as a big glove. Kids won't buy them."

The past two decades have seen a sharp increase in gimmickery in glove design, inspired largely, I suspect, by the need to generate sales rather than by the desire to improve the nation's fielding. Some of this activity may be an outgrowth of stepped-up competition from Japanese manufacturers. I like the story about the genesis of the special slot in the back of the gloves to permit the index finger to hang out:

Sometime in the 1950s, Yankee catcher Yogi Berra injured the index finger on his left hand. To spare the tender digit some of the pounding it would take inside the catcher's mitt, Yogi slipped it outside and continued to catch. The finger felt so good out there in the air and sunshine that Yogi did not bother to put it back into the mitt after it had healed. Other American

League catchers, sensing that the perennial MVP winner had discovered some arcane method for eliminating passed balls, quickly pulled their fingers from the mitt in imitation.

Today the practice has become endemic at all positions. Glovemakers have helped institutionalize it by providing a special slot for the superfluous finger. I suppose they had to. No kid would be found dead with five fingers thrust into a baseball glove. Unless, of course, he had been born with six.

For years I've been listening to loose talk (from fans, naturally) about the star-wars advance in glove design and how it has revolutionized fielding. The thing I hear most is that when manufacturers introduced the webbed pocket trap for fielder's gloves in the 1960s, it turned the game of baseball around. Every man on the field takes the ball in the webbing now, they tell me excitedly, just the way the first baseman has always done.

Who are they kidding? The rankest sandlotter knew about that technique half a century ago. In the old days, when a kid was drafted to play first and he didn't own a first baseman's mitt, he simply folded his fielder's glove diagonally and pulled his hand halfway out of the glove so that it rested lightly on the upper part of his fingers. (Usually, he had removed most of the padding anyway.) Outfielders often did the same thing. Middle infielders preferred to jam their hands well into the glove so that they could feel the ball. I wonder how often manufacturers have been responding to fashion rather than creating it?

To get some perspective on the matter of innovation in glove design, I talked with Rollie Latina, senior staff designer at Rawlings. Rollie's father, Harry "Bud" Latina, known for many years as "the Glove Doctor," started de-

signing baseball gloves for Rawlings back in 1922. Rollie
joined his dad in the operation in 1947, and took over as
top designer in 1960, when the elder Latina retired.

I asked Rollie Latina what lay down the road for baseball gloves. "Hard to say," he said. "There's been so
doggone much going on in the last ten years, it's kind of
tough to come up with anything better than what we've
got."

I also asked him what he thought was the most significant development in glove design in the past eighty years
or so. His answer surprised me. "Probably the Edge-U-
Cated Heel patent," he said. "That goes back to about
1959. Before that all the gloves had a big, wide-open heel
and there was never any actual snugging action of the
glove on the hand. In other words it was more or less
loose. The Edge-U-Cated Heel brought the sides of the
glove into the contours of the hand and the wrist and the
glove actually stayed on your hand better that way."

After I had thought about it for a minute, it made real
sense. I remembered the way a line drive, if you happened to take it on the thumb, might spin the glove
around on your hand. There used to be a big lump of padding in the heel, which mostly covered your wrist, where
it was not needed. The glove was held on by a thin strap
at the back. Occasionally, you would hear of an infielder
getting his glove torn off by a hard smash. How easy it is
to forget those things.

Latina assured me that his shop held no special brief for
big gloves, only good gloves. He said that Rawlings will,
and indeed does, make small gloves for major leaguers.
Glove size and style, he reminded me, is a matter of personal taste. Latina conceded that there might be difficulties in mass marketing smaller gloves.

I have long had a peculiar reaction to baseball gloves.

Whenever I see one, I also see inside it a dexterous human hand, the awesome product of fifty million years of evolution, just twitching to get out. I get the feeling that the hand craves contact with the ball. Watch a coach at first or third sometime when a ground foul is hit in his direction, especially if he's a former infielder, like Ed Brinkman, Dal Maxvill, or Ruben Amaro. Do they ever simply let the foul skip by to be retrieved by the ball girl? Never. And note how lovingly, how deftly they make the bare-handed scoop even on balls that are hit rather sharply. Often they fondle the ball for a second or two before returning it to the field. It sets me to wondering sometimes if maybe Bid McPhee and Fred Dunlap in their reluctance to don gloves were privy to some ancient truth about the affinity of the naked human hand for a baseball quite apart from the incidental pain to be endured.

Back in the late 1950s, at Pittsburgh's vast Forbes Field, Willie Mays pursued a drive from the bat of Roberto Clemente. It was headed for the base of the light tower in deepest left center field, about 450 feet from home plate. As Willie miraculously closed with the path of the ball, he reached out instinctively with his bare hand in a last best effort to intercept it. He made the catch.

Watching from high up in the grandstand, Pirate general manager, Branch Rickey, who up to that time may have attended between four and five thousand major-league games in his career, declared that Mays's catch was the greatest he had ever seen. No one on the Giants recalled having seen Willie make a better one, including his famous catch off Vic Wertz in the 1954 World Series. Curiously, when Willie came back to the dugout, he still had the ball clasped in his hand.

If it was the greatest catch that Branch Rickey ever saw and the greatest catch that Willie Mays ever made, it is conceivable that it was the greatest catch that *anyone* has ever made.

Bare-handed.

Think about that.

HENRY CHADWICK. Looking like an Old Testament prophet, "Father" Chadwick points to the irrefutable evidence of his famous black scoring book. "It took a bad hop," the culprit whines. "Not in my book," Chadwick thunders. *(National Baseball Library, Cooperstown, N.Y.)*

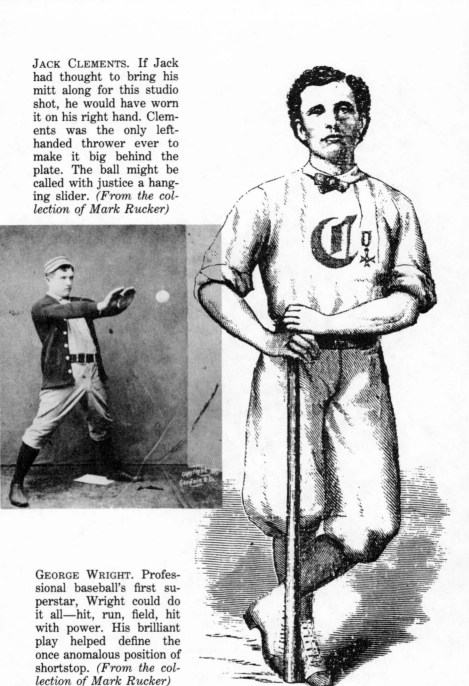

JACK CLEMENTS. If Jack had thought to bring his mitt along for this studio shot, he would have worn it on his right hand. Clements was the only left-handed thrower ever to make it big behind the plate. The ball might be called with justice a hanging slider. *(From the collection of Mark Rucker)*

GEORGE WRIGHT. Professional baseball's first superstar, Wright could do it all—hit, run, field, hit with power. His brilliant play helped define the once anomalous position of shortstop. *(From the collection of Mark Rucker)*

JAMES G. FOGARTY. Most baseball "action" shots of the nineteenth century were studio poses. Philadelphia's great ball hawk Jim Fogarty affects what was called the stork position. If you haven't guessed, the ball was hung from a wire. *(General Research Division, the New York Public Library, Astor, Lenox, and Tilden foundations)*

WILLIAM MITCHELL NASH. Billy Nash's teammate, pitcher Charles "Old Hoss" Radbourn, must have been scheduled for a photo session on the same morning and volunteered to play daring base runner so that the slick-fielding third baseman could demonstrate his block-and-tag technique for the camera. *(From the collection of Mark Rucker)*

ADRIAN "CAP" ANSON. An ancient camera captures a scene that must have been all too common at Chicago's West Side Grounds. Anson confirmed the oldest axiom of baseball eligibility: If you can hit, you can play. *(From the collection of Mark Rucker)*

MICHAEL JOSEPH GRIFFIN. In a rare outfield action shot from the early 1890s, perhaps taken in Brooklyn, the sure-handed Griffin makes ready to gather one in. Mike's confidence seems not at all threatened by the smallness of his glove. *(From the collection of Mark Rucker)*

The left fielder in this nineteenth-century schoolboy game
has clearly gotten a good jump on the ball. His effort may
be partly wasted, however, since in the custom of the age
his teammates are acting like spectators—no one ready for
a relay, no one backing up on the play. *(Culver Pictures)*

JOHN "BID" MCPHEE. The last of the bare-handed middle infielders, McPhee may have been the best fielding second baseman of the last century. *(National Baseball Library, Cooperstown, N.Y.)*

WILLIAM "BUCK" EWING. Ewing became New York's first baseball idol in a tradition that would continue with Mathewson, Ruth, DiMaggio, Mays, Mantle, Jackson, and others. Note Buck's two gloves—padded mitt for the left hand, fingerless glove for the throwing hand. This may have been a general practice among catchers prior to the appearance of the Decker patent mitt in the 1890s. *(Courtesy of the New York Historical Society, New York City)*

JOHN "HONUS" WAGNER. Pittsburgh's legendary "Flying Dutchman" appears a study in concentration, the mark of most great athletes. It's a fair bet that Honus was up on his toes for every pitch during his long career. *(National Baseball Library, Cooperstown, N.Y.)*

TRISTRAM E. SPEAKER. Before the era of DiMaggio and Mays, Tris was baseball's "Mr. Center Field." No center fielder in history has played as close behind second as Speaker did, but there's little doubt that today's lively ball and free-swinging mania would force the Gray Eagle a lot closer to the fence. *(National Baseball Library, Cooperstown, N.Y.)*

FIVE
Baseball's Masked Marvels

"You gotta have a catcher. If you don't, you're gonna see a lot of passed balls."
—CASEY STENGEL
Explaining New York Mets' first-round draft choice

THE CATCHER IS BASEBALL'S PREEMINENT DEfensive player. The fact is blazoned right in his title. Regardless of what other talents he has, he must, above all, be able to catch the ball. And he does this under the most difficult circumstances—batters swinging through the pitch, burly runners bearing down on the plate, pop fouls drifting toward the opponent's dugout. Only the shortstop is looked to for equally sure hands.

Beyond receiving 90-mph fastballs, sliders, screwballs, knucklers, and, occasionally, spitballs, the catcher is expected to throw with quickness and accuracy to all bases, to block wild pitches, to field balls hit in front of the plate, to catch anything hit into the air behind the plate, to back up first base on balls hit to the infield, and to make the toughest putout in the game—a tag play at home. On most teams he is expected to call the game, steady the pitcher, and position the defense. If when he has the mask off he's banging out twenty-five homers and driving in a hundred runs, his manager's wife and children will be sure to mention him in their nightly prayers. But this is gravy. A catcher's first job is catching.

It's a wonder that anyone ever masters enough skills to catch in the majors. In fact, most front-office people concede that year in and year out it remains the toughest position to fill satisfactorily. To make matters worse, it is not a job widely coveted by young players today, even when it looks like the quickest route to the big leagues. San Francisco scout Babe Barberis told me that after good hands and a strong throwing arm, the quality he looks for in a catching prospect is enthusiasm for the position. It's an increasingly rare commodity.

Catching has not enjoyed a good press. For years kids have been hearing from their elders playful admonitions against taking up the "tools of ignorance." When Herold "Muddy" Ruel, who caught with distinction through nineteen American League seasons, coined the expression back in the 1920s, it was clearly intended as lighthearted self-deprecation. An educated man and an off-season practicing lawyer, Ruel was known as an especially heady catcher. And it should be noted that Muddy specified ignorance, not stupidity.

Obviously, a catcher cannot be dumb if he is to be effective. By tradition he is the team leader. A pitcher may be dumb, of course, and I would venture to say that more than a few have been, though they can still win. Oh, it's nice to have a smart pitcher, I suppose, but it's strictly a luxury. After all, others are paid to think for him. Besides, he has enough on his mind just rehearsing for TV commercials. A team might even survive a dumb first baseman, especially if he hits forty home runs a year. But dumb and catcher are contradictory terms.

If you don't believe that catchers are the intellectual elite of the game, let's try Branch Rickey and Connie Mack for starters. How about Paul Richards, Al Lopez, and Moe Berg? The book on Berg, the multilingual Princetonian and O.S.S. operative, was that he might know seven languages but he couldn't hit in any of them. Still, Moe parlayed his modest talents into a fifteen-year major-league career. That's dumb?

Yogi Berra, with priceless good humor, endures endless kidding about his malapropisms, mixed metaphors, and colorfully rendered folk wisdom. But never deceive yourself that Yogi is anything but an intelligent man and a sound baseball thinker. Hall of Fame catchers do not come with low IQs. Maybe on occasion Yogi slips a gear in diction or syntax. Big deal. If he had come into the world a deaf mute, like outfielder William Hoy or pitcher Luther Taylor, Yogi might today hold rank as baseball's premier sage. You must admit that rendered in sign, "It ain't over till it's over" is bound to have struck a dignified chord. And you can't quarrel with its substance.

When I was a kid, catching was downright popular. It may have been the influence of the Depression. The catcher commanded more equipment than anyone else (even if it did belong to the school or an American Legion post). He had the biggest glove. Materially he could lord it over the rest of us. My guess is that catching was popular before that, too, going all the way back to the earliest days of the game. To begin with, it has always called for guts to get behind the plate, even when catchers were standing fifty feet back. There may not have been fastballs then, but there had to be other hazards aplenty. How about the risk of covering home while all those hundreds of runs were being scored in a single inning?

However far back from the plate they started, catchers must have recognized early on that the closer they moved, the more they could contribute to the game. Certainly a few daring ones must have been tempted to creep forward. Ironically, just as catchers grew bolder, the pitching got faster. It was a perfect formula for split lips, chipped teeth, bruised chests, dislocated fingers, and occasionally a broken nose. Also a vehicle for machismo. Wounded receivers were bound to draw a wealth of sympathy from lady spectators. Cynics may say that it takes a lot of pretty smiles to compensate for a broken beak, but glamour had to be a principal attraction of catching in the early days.

Still, even among heroes, flesh has limits of endurance. Having been forced by the evolution of the game into such a vulnerable spot, it had to be expected that the more prudent catchers would yield to such expedients as stuffing padding inside their shirts to prevent bruises and wearing broad rubber bands around their mouths to cut down on split lips.

Hands remained the greatest source of concern. There is a tradition that Cincinnati catcher Doug Allison was the first professional ballplayer to use a rudimentary glove way back in 1869. Some baseball historians put in a claim for another catcher, New York's Nathan Hicks. Chances are that we will never positively identify the first desperate backstop to appeal to his local saddlemaker for protection against foul tips. But if he had to go to his grave unheralded, he had the satisfaction of being buried with fingers reasonably intact.

The first direct claim to catching with a padded glove was made by James "Deacon" White, who played for half a dozen major-league teams over a span of twenty-two years. Actually, Deacon may have extended his career by abandoning catching for third base about halfway along. Toward the end of his life, White told a writer that he had used a padded glove as early as 1872, when all other catchers were bare-handed.

If Deacon White was not the first big-league catcher to wear a glove, he probably was first to wear a mask. The catcher's mask was the brainchild of F. Winthrop Thayer, who captained the Harvard baseball team. Early in 1877, Thayer tapped undergraduate James Alexander Tyng to catch for the Crimson varsity. Apprehensive for his patrician nose and pearly incisors, Tyng declined the honor with a gentlemanly bow. By way of persuasion, Thayer invoked the name of the hated Yales. Tyng was firm. The desperate Thayer tried shame. Unmoved, Tyng chose dishonor over disfigurement.

Harvards are not easily deterred once they've set their minds to something. Convinced that Tyng had the best pair of hands in the Yard to handle his pitching staff (probably consisting of one), young Thayer commissioned a tinsmith to modify an ordinary fencing mask so that it could be used by a catcher. With his Newmanesque profile secure inside the new gadget, young Tyng took the field with alacrity in the season's opener on April 12. Baseball had taken a leap forward. Within a few years, catchers were universally masked.

Hearing about the highjinks over in Cambridge, Deacon White, then with the Boston Red Stockings and catching the great Al Spalding, decided that it was worth crossing the Charles to have a look. Although he was impressed with the concept, White concluded that the Thayer mask looked too much like a birdcage, and he reasoned that it might prove too clumsy for use in the professional game. According to his account, he commissioned a Boston iron-worker to construct a mask of different design, fashioned from steel wire. White described his mask as covering only the face and being held on by elastic straps that went around the head. He makes it sound like the conventional catcher's mask we all know. What casts a small shadow over White's story is that in February 1878, Thayer applied for and received a United States patent on his mask and it was subsequently manufactured in volume by New York's Peck & Snyder.

Stories like White's suggest that apart from the obvious physical risks, it must have been particularly exciting to be a catcher in those days. Baseball was resolving itself into essentially a duel between pitcher and batter, and the function and style of battery play were shifting yearly under a barrage of rule changes. For example, the so-called "battery errors"—for a walk, a wild pitch, a passed ball, a hit batter—were promulgated and rescinded twice between 1883 and 1889. What an opportunity for a bright and enterprising young catcher to lessen the impact of mercurial rule changes by pioneering new styles of play behind the plate. No doubt some did just that. There may have been a hundred subtle changes in the catcher's craft in those years that we will never know about.

Without doubt, the biggest adjustment catchers had to make a century ago was to the legalization of overhand pitching in 1884. The pitcher was still only fifty feet from the plate—they did not increase the distance until 1893—and you can bet that some of those husky farmboys were throwing smoke from day one. With the advent of gloves and masks in the 1870s, a few bold receivers—White claimed to be one of them—moved closer to the plate. But apparently most continued to allow themselves a bit of walking-around room until confined to the catcher's box by custom and the rules in the early 1900s. You can hardly blame the poor catcher for wanting to back off. There is a story that one of Cy Young's first regular receivers resorted to lining his mitt with a slab of raw beefsteak. After nine innings of treatment from Cy's hummer, that steak must have been ready for a side order of french fries.

The season of 1885 couldn't have been far along before it became evident that catchers were not going to survive fastball pitching without further protection. Padding in gloves increased until it culminated in the Decker patent in 1890—a thick, round mitt that became the prototype for catcher's gloves until the 1960s. Masks were strengthened. And before the decade was out, Detroit's Charlie Bennett, one of the National League's finest catchers, had developed the chest protector. It's ironic that Bennett, a man conscious of safety, should have had his career cut short by a bizarre railway accident, which cost him both his legs.

The matter of protecting the catcher from injury must have been on a lot of minds in those days. An advertisement in Reach's baseball guide cites the achievement of Cleveland's Charles "Chief" Zimmer, who caught 125 games in 1890, as evidence of the effectiveness of their equipment. It should have been a compelling ad. Catching that many games is a job well done in any era.

The surprise in the evolution of catcher's gear is that it took until 1907 before a receiver appeared on the field wearing shin guards. It's assumed that a few catchers had earlier worn padding of a sort under their stockings, but the Giants' personable, salty-tongued Roger Bresnahan was the first to wear shin and knee guards openly, an idea he borrowed from cricket. Possibly because of the association with the English game, Bresnahan initially took some good-natured razzing from the fans. But he had the last laugh. Now he could crawl into bed at night without having to apply Sloan's Liniment to throbbing shins.

Bresnahan is also credited with strengthening the mask to prevent the wire from bending in and injuring the catcher's eye. An enterprising fellow, Roger was. He also demonstrated his flair for public relations by pretending that he had been born in Ireland to increase his appeal among New York's militant Hibernians.

By the 1880s, catchers were beginning to attract the attention and affection of the fans that had earlier been reserved for pitchers and long-ball hitters. Maybe it was becoming apparent to the kranks (as the fans were then called) that to hold down this demanding position required not only a brave man but also a resourceful one.

The game's first genuine superstar, Mike "King" Kelly, began as a catcher although his glove work was something less than distinguished. Sold by Chicago to Boston for the then incomprehensible sum of ten thousand dollars (in today's baseball values something close to four million, I estimate) in 1887, Mike was valued principally for his hitting, his baserunning, and his baseball cunning. He is the father of the slide and even inspired a hit song of the 1880s: "Slide, Kelly, Slide."

In the "World Series" with the Browns in 1886, Mike called for a pitchout with the series-winning run at third— and muffed the toss. It took him almost sixteen years to pull his fielding average up to .900, and he often fell down unaccountably when stationed under a fly ball, a phenomenon that some writers attributed to Mike's inordinate fondness for medicinal spirits.

Despite his deficiencies with the glove, Kelly left his mark on the trade of catching. He was first to insist that the pitcher let the infielders as well as the catcher know what he was going to throw. He had a strong arm and, as a clever base runner himself, he knew how to improve the catcher's throwing game. Mike may also have been the first backstop to decoy runners from third by pretending that the relay was slow coming in, and he was not above extralegal shenanigans, such as leaving his mask on the plate to intimidate runners trying to score. The King was probably the first to endow catching with real glamour.

If Mike Kelly didn't have good hands, there were others, less colorful, perhaps, who did. There was Chief Zimmer, of course, and the ill-starred Charlie Bennett. Washington's "Tall Tactician," Connie Mack, didn't have a long playing career but was highly respected. In this period also, Albert "Doc" Bushong, who played with several teams, reached the height of his popularity with the perennial American Association champions, the St. Louis Browns. A great favorite was the New York Giants' amiable William "Buck" Ewing, who actually caught in less than half of his 1,300 major-league game appearances but still surfaces occasionally on someone's all-time team as catcher. Buck is widely credited with being the first to catch from a crouch and became famous for his snap throw from that posture.

If stolen base totals is reliable evidence, Kelly's generation did not throw very effectively. Before 1900 it was not uncommon for teams to steal between 400 and 500 bases in a 135-game season. No, we can't really lay it on the pitchers this time, much as I would love to do so. The present balk rules were not put into effect until 1899, and before that it was common practice for a pitcher to feint a runner back to the base just before delivering the pitch. Then, for no apparent reason, and before the new balk rules were instituted, stolen bases started to decline. The only conclusion you can draw is that catchers were throwing better; they were learning the business. There is evidence that a few brave ones were playing closer to the plate, too, but we can't be sure who, or how close.

I can't find evidence of how well he could catch and throw, but if you're talking about durability behind the plate, the name of one of King Kelly's contemporaries comes to mind; the indestructible James "Deacon" McGuire. (Deacon, incidentally, seems to have been a standard nickname for a ballplayer who did not drink. That explains why few were so named.) McGuire played twenty-six seasons for eleven different teams in three major leagues and caught more than 1,600 games, a considerable feat then or now. Even today's vitamin-fed receivers normally look to careers of not more than 1,300 to 1,500 games, and Al Lopez's record of 1,918 outings behind the plate looks as secure as Gehrig's consecutive-game playing streak. McGuire was one of the first to make catching an exclusive role. Ewing, Kelly, and others played a variety of positions. Maybe Deacon actually liked catching.

It was around the turn of the century that organized baseball appears to have settled on the convention of catchers being right-handed throwers. As a fan I see no obvious reason why a lefty shouldn't catch. There's nothing to keep him from throwing to all bases, and he might even make the tag at the plate more easily. No doubt the answer lies in some subtleties of the catcher's craft not apparent from the stands, which have been discovered through trial and error.

There have been a few left-handed catchers. The Phillies' Jack Clements caught more than a thousand National League games—and he even played some shortstop and third base. Left-handers Fergy Malone, Pop Tate, and

Tom Doran also caught, but only token amounts. In 1958, in the last instance on record, the Cubs' left-handed first baseman, Dale Long, caught in a couple of games without harm to himself or the team.

Speaking of convention, not until the 1890s was it regular practice for the catcher to signal the pitcher what to throw. I must draw from this evidence the horrifying conclusion that until then pitchers were calling their own games. It's a wonder we don't have examples of opposing teams managing to lose the same ball game.

When you ask who was the all-time best catcher, there seems to be less agreement than for any other position. You can reel off a dozen names—Bresnahan, Kling, Schalk, O'Neill, Cochrane, Dickey, Hartnett, Ferrell, Lopez, Campanella, Berra, Bench—and find that each has a sizable constituency. Honus Wagner, who maintained an active connection with baseball until his death in 1955, said that no one matched the Cubs' sure-handed Johnny Kling. Ty Cobb, who died in 1961 and who was never distinguished for enlightened views on race, decided that the Dodgers' Roy Campanella was the best catcher he had ever seen. I remember octogenarians almost coming to blows in the endless New York debate over whether Buck Ewing or Roger Bresnahan was the greatest receiver of all time. They dismissed out-of-hand young whippersnappers like Cochrane, Dickey, and Hartnett.

Even up to the present, Bresnahan may have been named to more all-time teams than anyone else. I confess that I am always a little suspicious of an athlete who played in New York being named all-time anything, since the Big Apple was and is the hype capital of the world—first in newspapers, now on TV and in magazines. I'm sure that Bresnahan was good in his time. His fielding stats can stand with anyone's, and he handled great pitchers like Mathewson and McGinnity. But the "Duke of Tralee" was full of blarney, and there's no telling how he worked the susceptible New York press. The most curious thing about Bresnahan is that he was so fast John McGraw used him as lead-off man. Physically, Roger was built like a floor safe. Amazing.

Why is slowness afoot endemic among catchers, regardless of size? A catcher has to be smart, yes. No divine fiat says that he must be slow. But through the years most have been. Maybe it's all that squatting. Anyway, a few seasons back, Kansas City's John Wathan just about won himself a saliva test by stealing thirty-six bases. It was the most by a catcher since the White Sox's Ray Schalk stole thirty in 1916. And it also topped Bresnahan's thirty-four in 1903.

Lou Criger, a fine catcher for the Boston Red Sox early in this century, has sometimes been labeled the prototype lead-footed catcher. But if Lou couldn't steal bases himself, he wasn't going to let anyone else steal either. He may have been the first of baseball's rifle-armed catchers, and his favorite victim was the fleet-footed and irascible Ty Cobb. There's a story that the frustrated Cobb made a special project of successively stealing second, third, and home against Criger (or the pitcher) and loudly announcing his intention before each steal. Once Cobb's amourpropre had been suitably salved, Criger went back to throwing him out regularly.

As testimony that catchers have long been valued first for their hands and then for their bats, Criger compiled a lifetime batting average of .221 in an era when Cobb, Jackson, and Lajoie were topping .400. The White Sox's smooth-fielding Billy Sullivan, who played at the same time, batted only .212 for a sixteen-year career. But the most compelling example is the Dodgers' Bill Bergen, who pounded the ball at a .170 clip through almost a thousand games. No, that isn't a typo. It was rumored that Brooklyn manager Patsy Donovan made Bergen carry a diagram of the diamond for guidance in case he should ever get on base. In eleven years of play, Bill barely matched Hack Wilson's RBI total for a single season. With that kind of run production, Bergen must have been a phenomenon behind the plate. As a matter of fact, he had 202 assists one season, which says that there was nothing wrong with his arm.

The subject of catchers' throwing arms hardly ever fails to evoke the name of Jimmy Archer, who succeeded Johnny Kling with the old Chicago Cubs. Old-timers used to compare Archer's arm to everything but a laser beam, and only because lasers hadn't been invented yet. Archer was a marvelous fielder, too, carrying on a Cubs tradition established by Kling and continued by men like Bob O'Farrell, Gabby Hartnett, Clyde McCullough, and Randy Hundley. Chicago must be catchers country. The White Sox have had Sullivan, Schalk, Luke Sewell, Mike Tresh, Sherm Lollar, and Carlton Fisk.

When I was a teenager, the debate among sportswriters and fans alike about who was the best catcher centered on the Yankees' Bill Dickey and Detroit's Mickey Cochrane. Many Chicago fans put in a strong claim for the jovial Gabby Hartnett, and on the periphery there were dissident groups supporting candidates like Jimmie Wilson, then closing out his great career with the Phillies, Brooklyn's Al Lopez, once described to me by Red Barber as "perhaps the slickest fielding catcher I've ever seen," Sewell, and the much traveled Rick Ferrell. Among old-timers you might find a few sentimental votes for Cleveland's Steve O'Neill or Bob O'Farrell. Dickey and Cochrane were outstanding hitters as well as superb catchers, and that fact was bound to tip the balance heavily in their favor. Of course, Hartnett was a good hitter, too.

Although I was not of an age to make sound judgments in such matters, I went ahead and made them anyway. I was convinced that Cochrane was the greatest thing ever to pick up a catcher's mitt. He was easy and graceful in his movements, fast on his feet, and had an excellent arm. He was tenacious and glue-handed under a pop foul. I recall that one of the New York papers—maybe it was *The World-Telegram*—ran a full page of pictures of catchers' hands without identifying the owners in the cutline. It was an array of disjointed, gnarled claws, bearing witness to honorable struggles with a thousand and one foul tips. One pair, however, displayed long, tapered fingers that might have belonged to Vladimir Horowitz. Yes, they were Cochrane's, and I suspect that the evidence was enough to cement my opinion. Black Mike had soft, sure hands, but there was nothing else soft about him. Anyway, that was before I had seen Jim Hegan or Johnny Bench, and so I have learned to reserve judgment.

It was also before I had matured enough to take a closer look at Bill Dickey, who may have suffered in my judgment from familiarity, since he played with a local team. Moreover, Bill made catching look so easy that it was hard for a kid to know how good he really was. For a time I actually thought that the Yankees were carrying him for his hitting, which many teams might have been happy to do even if he had hands of stone.

Except through the testimony of writers and players, it is hard for the average fan to assess how well a catcher knows the league's hitters and handles the pitcher. My favorite story about how thorough Dickey's "book" was comes from *Washington Post* baseball writer Shirley Povich. During World War II, Povich was in a hotel elevator with the Yankee catcher when a young army corporal who had played briefly in the American League some years earlier stepped into the car. Seeing Dickey, the soldier said, "Hello, Bill, you probably wouldn't remember me." "Sure, I do," Dickey said. "We used to pitch you high and inside." But he had to ask the corporal his name.

Dickey's single shortcoming—it should come as no surprise—was lack of foot speed, though he was nimble enough behind the plate. Naturally, it placed him squarely in the grand tradition, especially among his contemporaries. In fact, compared to some catchers of his era, Bill was another Hermes.

Gus Mancuso, for example, a smallish man and a good journeyman receiver for some pennant-winning Giant and Cardinal teams, stole only eight bases in almost 1,400 games. Cincinnati's Ernie Lombardi required an additional 200 games to match Gus on the base paths. But at 230-plus pounds, maybe Big Lom had an alibi. I can't verify this, but friends from the Middle West have told me that Cincinnati newspapers were known to drop Ohio River floods to page two and run a seventy-two-point banner proclaiming: LOMBARDI GOES FROM FIRST TO THIRD ON A SINGLE TO RIGHT.

That's nothing. In a comparable number of games, the Phillies' Spud Davis stole fewer bases than either Mancuso or Lombardi. In fact, in his last ten years in the majors, Spud stole only once. There's a story that at contract time his general manager pointed to it as evidence that Davis might be slowing down.

It wasn't so much the glacial baserunning that characterized the catchers of the 1930s as the infrequency of lateral movement behind the plate. At bat Lombardi was a standing threat to the integrity of the outfield walls; in the mask and pads he metamorphosed into inoffensive statuary. If they had given a trophy for passed balls, Lom would have won permanent possession before he was halfway through his career.

Then there was the Giants' Frank "Shanty" Hogan, who claimed that his bathroom scale read 240 before breakfast and without his socks on. But Shanty may have left his glasses off along with his socks at the weigh-in. In today's economy it might take Gary Carter's salary just to feed him. It was said that the club's traveling secretary would faint when the catcher turned in his dinner checks. But I can attest that it is not true that a pop foul had to be hit at least three hundred feet in the air to give Shanty a chance to get under it. Let's just say that fans at the Polo Grounds felt more comfortable with that sort of margin. Shanty, incidentally, had no peer at blocking the plate.

There were others dropped from the same mold. Brooklyn's Babe Phelps, known to the Flatbush Faithful as "Blimp," wanted to give the lie to the hoary charge that catchers couldn't hit their own weight. It might have made him batting champion. In the case of the itinerant "Jolly Rollie" Hemsley, it certainly wasn't size that immobilized him. He wasn't that bulky by the standards of the day. One writer said that Rollie was living proof that bourbon may lend wings to the spirit but not to the heels. Then there was Washington's Cliff Bolton, who was small of stature and, as far as anyone knew, abstemious. The betting was that Cliff was the only man in baseball who would lose to Gus Mancuso in a foot race.

To this day receivers are not burning up the base paths, but we have seen prodigies of sound catching since World War II—some dazzling, a lot just plain excellent, the bulk journeyman solid. Who can forget Brooklyn's Roy Campanella shifting his fireplug bulk with such agility that it was sometimes startling to witness? And there was

Cleveland's elegant Jim Hegan, the Yankees' inelegant but nonetheless wonderful Yogi Berra, and the White Sox's nearly flawless Sherm Lollar; the two Dels—the Cardinals' Del Rice and the Braves' Del Crandall; Cincinnati's Johnny Edwards and Detroit's Bill Freehan; Thurman Munson, the Yankees' diamond in the rough; the Mets' intense Jerry Grote and the Cubs' volatile Randy, Hundley; the uncannily graceful Johnny Bench, who has virtually rewritten the book on catching; the Red Sox's regal Carlton Fisk, Texas's sturdy Jim Sundberg, Philadelphia's cerebral Bob Boone, and the reigning Gary Carter and Lance Parrish; the industrious journeymen, Gus Triandos and Tom Haller; Cleveland's hard-luck Ray Fosse. There are probably more.

I kid about mountainous Shanty Hogan and "Schnozz" Lombardi, but the catching crop of recent years has been less than anorectic. On the whole they are probably larger than the old-timers. My guess is that Johnny Edwards would fill out Shanty's velvet smoking jacket very nicely. Kansas City's Fran Healy, one of the fastest catchers of this century, might even split a seam.

The best catcher since World War II? Oh no, I'm not going to walk into that one. When I was fifteen I might have been brash enough, but not now. Age has taught me how little I know about catching. Like any fan, I am conscious of the obvious things—throwing, lateral movement, blocking the plate, running down pop fouls. What I can't know for sure unless an inside observer tells me is how well a catcher handles the pitchers, learns the hitters, and oversees the defense.

I assume that even after 150 years, the craft of catching is still evolving. For the workhorse behind the plate there must always be new tricks to learn. I remember being surprised to read that the White Sox's Hall of Famer Ray

Schalk, who played as recently as the mid-1920s, pioneered the practice of backing up first base to guard against overthrows from the infield. It's something you would have expected to originate with Deacon White or Buck Ewing. The speedy, ubiquitous Schalk sometimes made putouts at second, and he also stole 176 bases in his career.

To me the most obvious change in catching in the past thirty years is the one-handed style, made possible by the introduction of the flexible mitt in the 1960s, and brought to perfection by Johnny Bench. Oh, it's probably a form of hot-dogging, I know, and in fact I deplore one-handed catches by outfielders. But the way these young receivers pick up—with what Arnold Hano describes as "the beauty of nonchalance"—low pitches that might have been passed balls in the old days is hard to resist. And, on the plus side, the new style must certainly cut down on injuries to the meat hand.

I like to assume that most catchers are still calling the games. Nevertheless, the existence of computers, elaborate performance charts, and pitchers with agents makes me nervous. I hope that one of the catcher's oldest and most important functions is not ticketed for extinction. It would be a move toward robbing the game of whatever romance is left. They have taken away the sunshine, the doubleheaders, the grass, the cozy parks, meat from the hot dogs, and hops from the beer. It's not a lot of comfort at this point, but thank God no plastic-obsessed genius has designed a computer that can catch the ball.

No discussion of sure-handed catching would be complete without a special nod to the unique Lawrence Peter Berra. Young fans are probably not aware of this, but Yogi had to learn the catching trade from square one after he arrived in the majors from the navy in 1946. After watching Berra struggle through a 1947 World Series game, even the kindly Connie Mack was moved to describe it as "the worst exhibition of catching I have ever seen."

But Berra persevered and the Yankees recalled Bill Dickey from retirement to, in Yogi's words, "learn me all his experience." Dickey "learned" the young catcher well. In a few years Yogi was to help lead the Yankees to thirteen more pennants and himself to win the Most Valuable Player Award three times. Perhaps most remarkable of all, between July 28, 1957, and May 10, 1959, he caught 148 games without an error. Think of 950 chances without letting a base runner advance on an overthrow, without dropping a windblown pop fly, without letting the ball be kicked away by some gorilla trying to score. Yes, it's still a record.

Casey Stengel, who may have been experiencing a touch of linguistic empathy, offered the final word on Yogi's catching: "Maybe he can't say it good," Casey declared, "but he can do it."

SIX

Sweeping the Corners

"I prefer third base because it's a glamour position."
—WADE BOGGS
In response to the suggestion that he move to first base

I T HAS LONG BEEN A CUSTOM IN BASEBALL TO POST sluggers with weak gloves at first and third on the supposition that stone hands at the corners are likely to do little substantive damage. I think that's a big mistake. With division titles often decided by one-run margins, and third basemen handling up to 400 chances a season, first basemen up to 1,400, the opportunities for mischief are abundant.

Well then, someone is certain to ask, where else do you shelter the butter-fingered, good-natured oaf who can hit twenty home runs a year? Good question. How about Double-A? The early retirement list? Your friendly local carwash?

Oh, I know that such comments reveal me for what I am, a crochety old fan who has watched maybe a thousand ball games and thinks he has discovered a truth that has been eluding managers ever since Harry Wright took his Cincinnati whiz kids on tour in 1869. But it should be obvious. A team can't afford a porous glove at any position. Why, then, don't real-life managers see it my way? Because no manager in the history of the universe will ever be convinced that he has enough hitting, not even when eight of his regulars are driving in two hundred runs apiece. It's a mind-set that comes with the territory. Why should a man who would ax-murder his sister in exchange for ten home runs a season scruple at putting a Neanderthaler at third or first who might deliver him twenty?

Don't get me wrong. I have compassion for managers. They wouldn't be the way they are if they didn't have to handle a pitching staff.

It might surprise Wade Boggs that long before he was born, not only was first base as glamorous as third, it may have been *the* glamour position. Consider that in the mid-1930s, half the first basemen now in the Hall of Fame were active players—Lou Gehrig, Bill Terry, Jimmie Foxx, Hank Greenberg, Jim Bottomley, and Johnny Mize. Add Buck Leonard of the Negro leagues and it comes to more than half. For what it's worth I am convinced that at least three of their contemporaries, the Cubs' Charlie Grimm, Cincinnati's Frank McCormick, and Washington's Joe Kuhel, belong in Cooperstown with them—and in time that could happen.

Back in those days, a first baseman was a first baseman. No one would mistake him for anything else. It was a pro-

fession in itself, a life-style. None of this business of re-
cycling outfielders who can't throw, catchers with tired
thigh muscles, third basemen with no range. (In those
days, third basemen had no range anyway.) A strapping
lad would show up at spring training carrying a first baseman's mitt, and if he made the grade he would probably
find himself playing 150 games a season at first for the
next ten to fifteen years. Every team, it seemed, had a
regular first baseman. No one had to ask: Who's on first?

When kids waited outside the players' entrance after
the game seeking autographs, there was never a problem
spotting the first baseman, even if you didn't know him
on sight. He was always the biggest, most rugged guy,
the RBI man—Gehrig, Greenberg, Foxx—the one you
wished was your older brother after the Boy Scout Coun-
cil had perversely shifted your troop meeting place to the
far side of the railroad tracks. Even first basemen who
were distinguished for their slick fielding and agility—
Terry, Grimm, McCormick—sprang from the same mold
physically. McCormick was six feet four and weighed
about 210. Today we have shortstops that size—and first
basemen who are five feet ten. It's a different world now.
You definitely need a scorecard.

In the old days, there was a popular image of the third
baseman, too, though not as often realized in the flesh as
in the case of first base. A proper third baseman was seen
as ectomorphic, tall and lean, preferably with a bit of a
swagger. A western-sheriff type with spikes instead of
spurs. There was all that business about "the hot corner,"
even though a cursory look at the stats would have shown
that on average a third baseman handled fewer than three
chances a game, including bunts and slow rollers. Let me
hasten to add that with guys like DiMaggio, Foxx, and
Lombardi on the loose, a third baseman was not entirely

without risk of decapitation. Still, the odds were in his favor.

I guess the Cubs' genial Stan Hack came closest to an earthly manifestation of the ideal third baseman of the day. Tall, slender, handsome, confident, Hack was the idol of every sandlot urchin playing third in a pair of torn knickers. I never saw Stan swagger, but it would have been forgivable in his case. He was fast, aggressive, graceful. A lifetime .300 hitter, he sported a glove of twenty-four-karat gold. Don't ask me why he isn't in the Hall of Fame.

At the other end of the scale physically, but still playing a pretty fair third, was the White Sox's pear-shaped playing manager, Jimmy Dykes. In between was an assortment of sizes and shapes. What many had in common, alas, was an absence of swift lateral movement. But I doubt that anyone noticed. I can't remember seeing a third baseman actually leave his feet to dive for a hard smash until sometime in the 1950s. I'm not saying that none ever did. I just never saw it.

When I think about it, every position had its powerful mystique in the old days, even left field. Goose Goslin was a left fielder. You could tell just by looking at him. So were the Giants' Joe Moore and the Cardinals' Ducky Medwick. A left fielder looked like a left fielder even if he had on a camel's hair sports jacket. Or so we believed. Now we live in an age of platoon players. A bullpen catcher leaving for the ball park can't be sure he won't wind up playing shortstop that night. Last night I watched a game on TV. The home team had outfielders at first and third, its regular shortstop in center, its center fielder in left. Maybe it's more efficient this way, but it robs the positions of charm.

Because of the character of the game, first base must

have acquired a special aura from the earliest days. Action there was assured regardless of the general pace of the game. Runners had to be thrown out. It was axiomatic from the time of Old Reliable Joe Start that a first baseman's chief function was to catch throws from the other infielders and the catcher—any kind of throws—and remember to keep his foot on the bag. Going into the hole, guarding the line, being cutoff man, making the 3–6–3 double play—all this was to come later and become frosting on the cake.

It must not have taken long for someone to discover that it was advantageous to have a big man at first to serve as a target. Joe Start was small, but his successor as Mr. First Base, Cap Anson, was about the size of Baltimore's Boog Powell. The resemblance ends there. Powell was an excellent fielder.

I probably pick on old Cap too much, but he seems to me a perfect example of the halo effect. Because he hit .333 over a twenty-two-year career, a parallel legend sprang up that Anson was a great first baseman. There's not much in the record or in contemporary testimony to support it. I realize that the old bird probably played the first half of his career without a glove and I try to heed Red Barber's admonition to judge a player in his own time. Cap may have caught most of what was thrown to him. And he may even have introduced the long stretch, as is claimed for him. But he bobbled a shocking number of baseballs even when measured against his contemporaries. Anson may not have been the worst first baseman of his era, but I am sure that he was not the best.

If I had to name the best first baseman of the Victorian era on evidence available—and it is scanty—I would have to say the Giants' Roger Connor. A left-handed thrower, Connor was as large as Anson, but by all accounts significantly more agile and sure-handed. Some believe that "Big Roger" probably inspired the team's nickname. Like Anson, Connor is in the Hall of Fame, and like Anson he's there because he was a heavy hitter. Connor happens to have been an excellent fielder as well, not as imaginative and daring at first base as his contemporary, Charlie Comiskey, perhaps, but steady and reliable.

A studio-posed "action" photo of Connor taken as late as 1887 shows him not wearing a glove. I can't determine whether he ever wore one. Judging from the size of his hands, he didn't need one. If you tanned Roger's right hand and tied a thong around the fingers, it could pass for the fielder's glove your kid got last Christmas. The photo shows Connor catching a throw two-handed. It must have remained the custom among first basemen until fairly late.

Speaking of catching with two hands, I like the story about Cincinnati manager Pop Snyder who, in 1882, acting on the complaint of his shortstop, Chick Fulmer, fined first baseman Henry Luff five dollars for taking a throw one-handed. The indignant Luff quit the team. Who could blame him? At least he had caught the ball. Anson and others were dropping throws two-handed and probably drawing raises. The irony is that in time, the one-handed catch became *de rigueur* for first basemen.

Joe Start may have been first to demonstrate the advantage a left-handed thrower has in playing first, principally because a lefty doesn't have to turn his body when throwing to the other bases. I am surprised that the idea would have occurred to anyone back then. Playing for Chicago in 1878, Start accepted 732 chances, of which only 13 were assists. Some of his contemporaries had fewer. It's a wonder that his arm didn't atrophy from lack of use.

Many managers have disputed the theory that a left-hander has significant advantage when playing first, most recently Earl Weaver in his book on strategy. And the history of the game offers ample evidence that a right-hander can play the bag supremely well. To name just a few, the Philadelphia Athletics' Stuffy McInnis, the Cardinal's Ed Konetchy, Brooklyn's Gil Hodges, and, among active players, Baltimore's Eddie Murray. It's true, however, that most of the truly great first basemen have been lefties.

A left-handed first baseman who was less than poetry in motion, but nonetheless helped define the position in the early days, was Jake Beckley, who played for Pittsburgh, Cincinnati, and others in the 1890s and early 1900s. When you talk about first base you have to mention Jake because he played more games at the position than any man in history—2,377. Beckley made the Hall of Fame, doubtless on the strength of his hitting and longevity. Ironically, for many years Jake's was one of the few plaques at Cooperstown to mention an accomplishment in fielding, his record 23,696 putouts. I say ironically because he had the most outrageously inaccurate arm in baseball. When Jake cocked his arm, the story goes, the fans sitting behind third base instinctively ducked. So did the fans behind first. But first basemen didn't throw much in those days, so I guess it didn't matter.

It's funny the way fans and baseball broadcasters treat a poor arm as if it were a social disease or bad breath. They tend to skirt the subject, especially if a big star is concerned. As fine a fielder as Steve Garvey is, he doesn't have a good arm. But you would never know it without watching him over a period of time. No broadcaster would ever mention it. It reminds me of the case of Pittsburgh's Hall of Fame third baseman Pie Traynor, who used to be named to everyone's all-time team. I only saw Traynor play a few times toward the end of his career and could

form no judgment. But I have asked old-timers how good
he was. One, after looking about furtively to determine
who might be listening, told me, "Pie had no equal coming
in on a bunt, but he had a scatter arm. Kept first basemen
busy and he threw a lot of souvenir balls into the right-
field boxes." Others were vaguely laudatory. I read later
that teammate Max Carey always believed it was Traynor's throwing error that cost Pittsburgh the pennant in
1921.

I have no doubt that Traynor was light-years ahead of
his contemporaries at third because of his mobility and aggressive style of play. But the numbers confirm that he
was error-prone, and it's likely that many of his record
total of 324 errors were bad throws. I have a hunch that
one of today's managers might move Pie to first to take
advantage of his bat.

As regards first base, my research has failed to reveal
exactly when the stretching one-handed catch and the
smooth style of play that we so admire took hold. It seems
to have been well established by the time Hal Chase began his career with the New York Highlanders in 1905. A
good guess is that Fred Tenney of the Boston Beaneaters,
acknowledged the best fielding first baseman at the turn
of the century, helped popularize the style. One of the
first college players to turn professional (he had been a
left-handed catcher at Brown), Tenney, like Charlie Comiskey before him, was a thinking ballplayer and is credited
with perfecting, among other plays, the 3–6–3 double
play, still a delight to watch. Tenney had the advantage of
being able to work with the great Boston infield of Jimmy
Collins at third, Bobby Lowe at second, and Herman
Long at short, a group that refined and improved on the
defensive strategies of the notorious Baltimore Orioles.

Tenney may be best remembered for popularizing the

little pudding-style glove that was the prototype of today's first baseman's mitt and to which he gave his name.
No photo of the "tenney" shows me clearly whether the
glove had a webbing. It must have taken a brave man and
a sure hand inside a tenney to try a one-handed catch.

With the emergence of Hal Chase in the period before
World War I, the kind of first-base play still considered
the ideal came to full flower—nimble movement around
the bag, the graceful sweep of the glove when digging out
low throws or making a tag, the quick, hard, side-arm
throws to other bases. "Prince Hal" is an enigmatic figure
in the history of the game. Laid end to end, tributes to his
elegant fielding would stretch from Cooperstown to Las
Vegas, but his name will never be in the Hall of Fame
because he was barred from organized baseball in 1920 for
his flagrant gambling on games and the suspicion that
he often orchestrated the results. For a player of extraordinary natural gifts, he holds no significant fielding
records and made a surprising number of errors. His
defenders insist that Chase was ahead of his time and
that others were caught napping by the quickness of his
throws.

The St. Louis Browns' George Sisler succeeded to
Chase's crown, and there are still a few old fans around
who believe that "Gorgeous George" (a nickname he
couldn't possibly have escaped) has had no peer with the
glove. The left-handed Sisler was so good that his manager, Branch Rickey, sometimes played him at second and
third. In the early 1920s, Sisler suffered an illness that
almost cost him his sight, and both his hitting and fielding
fell to levels that would do ordinary men proud but which
were clearly non-Sislerian. Consequently, his lifetime
stats don't look as impressive as they might have under
more fortunate circumstances. That sounds odd when

you're talking about a guy with a .340 batting average over fifteen seasons. Sisler also tops all first basemen in total assists. That's how good George was.

Among Sisler's contemporaries, Brooklyn's Jake Daubert, Washington's Joe Judge, and the Athletics' Stuffy McInnis were top gloves at first and good hitters all. In fact, Daubert was, like Sisler, a two-time batting champion. It raises the eternal question: What do you have to do to get into the Hall of Fame? Daubert has the distinction of having played more than two thousand games at first base and never an inning at any other position.

In thinking over the best fielding first basemen I have watched in my lifetime, off the top of my head I would name Charlie Grimm, Bill Terry, Joe Kuhel, George McQuinn, Frank McCormick, Mickey Vernon, Wes Parker, Gil Hodges, Vic Power, Bill White, Ferris Fain, and George Scott. Active players I've omitted, since we don't yet know how good they will become. I remain convinced that Terry was the greatest. Maybe I should modify that to most pleasing to watch. It's like choosing a Nijinsky over a dozen Nureyevs, or a Nureyev over a dozen Nijinskys.

If I close my eyes I can still see "Memphis Bill" with his slouching, negligent air stretch at the last instant and gather in a throw, wide and in the dirt, with a casual flick of the wrist. He always appeared to be the only person in the park not worried on an errant toss, and I am sure that the fielding averages of a generation of Giant infielders are points above what they deserve to be. Terry was remarkably quick for such a big man. No less an authority than Joe DiMaggio credits him with perfecting the force at third on an attempted sacrifice, a play which still calls for steady nerves and perfect timing.

I was pleased to come across support for my view on

Terry in a book by the venerable Fred Lieb, who had watched all the great ones from Chase and Sisler up through the era of Scott and White. "Terry was the greatest first baseman I ever saw," Lieb writes, "with the possible exceptions of George Sisler and Hal Chase, when Hal was giving it his all."

I have never played first base unless it was in some long-forgotten softball game at an office picnic, and then surely under protest. Maybe out of this ignorance I exaggerate its difficulties. In an effort to get an answer, I turned to the dean himself, James Barton "Mickey" Vernon, who played more games at first base than anyone in history, except Jake Beckley, 2,237 in all. In addition to wearing one of the best gloves in baseball, Mickey was twice batting champion of the American League. "When they say that anyone can play first," Mickey said, "I add to that sentence in my mind 'but not well.' It takes much practice and a lot of knowing where to be at the right time. It takes growing up there. I guess some good athletes have made the adjustment to becoming first basemen, but they have worked at it. You have to work at it."

Mickey tells the story of the day in 1950 that Joe DiMaggio was pressed into service at first in a game at Washington's Griffith Stadium after returning from an injury. Yankee manager, Casey Stengel, wanted to spare Joe having to run in the outfield. During the game DiMaggio fell down once pursuing a grounder, got his feet tangled on another occasion, and generally had an unhappy time. After the game a reporter asked the Yankee Clipper if it was the first time he had ever played first base. Not only was it the first time, Joe replied wryly, it was the last. "And DiMaggio was the greatest all-round player I ever saw," Mickey adds.

It does seem to me that play at first has not improved

nearly as much as it has at the other positions, especially third and catcher. Looked at another way, this is saying that first-base play was already pretty good in the old days. I am reminded of men like Greenberg, Gehrig, Foxx, the Cardinals' Johnny Mize, Brooklyn's Dolf Camilli—big guys who were valued primarily for their long-ball hitting. They were not bad in the field. Let me put it positively. They were good in the field, especially Foxx, who could play a number of positions, and Camilli, a whiz at the cutoff.

Apparently, when Lou Gehrig reached the majors in 1925, his glove was more of a threat to the Yankees' fortunes than his bat was to the opposition's. Like other fence-busters of his era, he might easily have gotten by with taking a casual view of his responsibilities in the field. But Gehrig was one of the most earnest, hard-working athletes who ever lived. In his early years with the Yankees, he spent long hours working to improve his fielding, learning to maneuver around the bag. His managers and coaches noted that from spring training on, Lou was the first one on the field in the morning and the last one to leave. By the time I first saw him play in the 1930s, his play was short of Gold Glove quality, to be sure, but he was a solid, competent first baseman. I can't recall ever seeing Gehrig make a bad play.

There's a similar story about Hank Greenberg, who, when he reported to Detroit in the early 1930s, was a six-feet-four tanglefoot at first base. But Hank worked long and hard to turn himself into a better than average fielder. Then, in an act of unselfishness, Greenberg, one of baseball's premier stars, volunteered to learn to play the outfield so that the Tigers could get the granite-handed Rudy York's big bat into the lineup. There must have been times when he looked in from left field to watch York at first and felt like George Sisler in exile.

It would be nice if the race of regular first basemen were to reemerge as genuine career types. At present only Cecil Cooper, Chris Chambliss, Eddie Murray, Keith Hernandez, and Kent Hrbek seem to have been bred to the position from an early age. Steve Garvey and Dan Driessen, excellent as they are, had to be recruited from other positions. Given the current obsession with platooning and the ever-present menace of computers, I don't expect that in future we will witness the rise of a dozen Eddie Murrays. It would be a bit much, in fact, to expect even two Eddie Murrays. But you know what I mean.

Wade Boggs's assumptions about the glamour accruing to tenure at third are still as sound as a Krugerrand in a Swiss bank vault. When you stop to think about it, the aura that has grown up around the position is something of a paradox. In most games nothing much goes on over there. The great Yankee manager, Joe McCarthy, is supposed to have said that you can play third base sitting in a rocking chair. Please note that "Marse Joe" never went so far as to test the theory with any of his many pennant winners, but there may be something to what he says.

Frank Malzone confirms that the relative infrequency of action at the hot corner can be a threat to concentration. If you play the position properly, Frank says, you are supposed to be up on your toes 120 to 150 times a game, ready to move. When only two or three batted balls a game are likely to come your way, it takes a strong will to keep yourself alert on every pitch.

Yet Boggs is correct. There may be few chances at third, but they are often exhilarating chances. A guy hits a grassburner toward the hole, beyond the reach of your shortstop. With eyes shut and a prayer on your lips, you

stretch as far to the left as you can and—miracle. The
ball's in the webbing. The batter has scarcely taken three
strides. Now you are offered a luxury that never comes
the way of a shortstop going into the hole. You may
straighten and, for just the smallest fraction of a second,
pause to contemplate your helpless, scrambling victim before cutting him down with a perfect throw.

I wonder to what extent the need to keep your head in
the game and maintain a touch of humility have affected
the comings and goings at third base in recent years.
Much the same thing appears to be happening at third as
at first. There was a time when every team had a card-
carrying third baseman, a guy good for 150 games against
all kinds of pitching, who never seemed to get hurt
enough to be benched, players like Rolfe, Hack, Detroit's
Marv Owen, Washington's Pinky Higgins, Cleveland's
Ken Keltner, the Phillies' Pinky Whitney. A few were su-
perbly gifted with the glove, most would do you no grave
damage. Need I add that they all hit a ton. It was part
of the job description. A general manager would have
laughed at the idea of paying two salaries to man one position.

Now, I don't blame the manager for today's itinerant
labor at third. Put yourself in his place. Through the long
nights of January he warms his spirit with expectations of
finding a rookie with the glove of Aurelio Rodriguez and
the bat of Pedro Guerrero. But when he arrives at training camp in the spring he finds that the general manager
has signed a high-school phenom who has Pedro's glove
and Aurelio's bat. It means he must recall that reserve
outfielder he sent to Triple-A and pray that the opposition
doesn't know how to bunt.

Funny thing about third. Activity there actually has de-
creased in the past century. In the 1880s and 1890s it was

common for a third baseman to average well over four chances a game. A few topped five. It might have been all that bunting they used to do, except that it wasn't until Boston's Jimmy Collins came along in the late 1890s that it became the custom for the third baseman to charge bunts.

Whatever kind of chances Victorian third sackers were accepting, several managed to achieve star status. Chicago's Ned Williamson got loads of ink and was popular with the fans. He succeeded Cap Anson at third when Anson was named the White Stockings' manager in 1879. We don't have to speculate why Cap's first managerial decision was to move himself to first. Williamson must have had good hands. As he got older he was moved from third to short. When have you seen that switch before with a veteran infielder?

The St. Louis Browns' Arlie Latham was a high profile third baseman, too. Arlie was a bouncy, aggressive little guy and a whirlwind on the base paths, a kind of early-day Pepper Martin. The inside word is that he handled grounders like Pepper as well. In any case, Arlie contributed to the charisma long associated with third.

Consensus favorite for the slickest third baseman of the 1880s is Cincinnati's Warren "Hick" Carpenter. Hick was almost always among the league leaders in total chances and double plays, and he maintained a respectable fielding average. (In those days that meant the mid-.800s.) Ready for a shock? Carpenter was left-handed. Either Hick was phenomenally good or base runners in the American Association were phenomenally bad. Probably a bit of both.

A short while back, desperate to shore up the left side of his infield, White Sox manager Tony LaRussa was forced to play slick-fielding lefty first baseman Mike Squires at third. Mike got through forty or so innings unscathed until the front office had time to acquire Roy Smalley.

A close examination of the records persuades me that Billy Nash, Jimmy Collins's predecessor at Boston, may have been the best of the nineteenth-century third basemen. Billy's numbers would pass muster even by modern standards, and he was highly regarded by both the press and fans of the 1890s.

Ability to charge and handle bunts and topped balls has long been an important measure of a third baseman's value. Among speed merchants like Ty Cobb, it may have been the only measure. Cobb said of the White Sox's Buck Weaver, "He was the greatest third baseman I ever saw. There was no chance to beat out a bunt on him." Until the bunting game began to decline in the home-run atmosphere of the 1920s and 1930s, reputations of superstar third basemen, such as Collins, the Giants' Art Devlin, the Red Sox's Larry Gardner, Cincinnati's Heinie Groh, along with Weaver and Pie Traynor, rested a great deal on their success in smothering the bunt. Today, a third baseman is expected to do that and a lot more, particularly to range to his left.

As with most positions, it seems to take a very potent bat to get a third baseman into the Hall of Fame. You have to wonder whether even Brooks Robinson would have made it without his 286 homers. But now that they are admitting shortstops with lifetime batting averages of less than .320, maybe anything is possible.

In fairness to the beleaguered Cooperstown electors, the roll call of slick gloves at third is fairly lengthy. Most of these swung pretty good bats, too. Between the world wars, new glory was brought to the position by men like Pie Traynor, Washington's steady Ossie Bluege, Willie Kamm—the White Sox's challenge to Gene Kelly, the Yankees' "Jumping Joe" Dugan, Pinky Whitney, Stan Hack, Red Rolfe, Bill Werber, Ken Keltner, and perhaps

the most underrated of his generation, the Browns' hardworking, hard-hitting Harlond Clift.

Few rookies have arrived in the majors under more
pressure than Kamm. In 1923, the White Sox paid San
Francisco $100,000 for the young third baseman, and the
nation's sports writers fainted dead away. Just three
years earlier, the Yankees had paid only $25,000 more for
Babe Ruth, who was already the league's premier slugger—and that was considered outrageous. But young
Willie rode out the storm and led American League third
basemen in fielding for six straight seasons. He was a
timely, if not overpowering, hitter.

Since World War II, third-base play has been, I think,
excellent overall and in some instances nothing short of
magical. Names that come to mind immediately are Detroit's Hall of Famer George Kell, Brooklyn's acrobatic
Billy Cox, Frank Malzone, the Boyers (Ken of the Cardinals and Clete of the Yankees), the Phillies' much underrated Willie "Puddin' Head" Jones, Eddie Yost, San
Francisco's stylish Jim Davenport, the incomparable
Brooks Robinson, Houston's Doug Rader, the Phillies'
Don Money; more recently, the Cardinals' Ken Reitz, Detroit's Aurelio Rodriguez, the Yankees' Graig Nettles,
Philadelphia's Mike Schmidt, Texas's Buddy Bell, and I'm
sure I have forgotten several more.

Technically, I can claim to have watched Kamm,
Traynor, and Bluege, but at an age when I was more interested in the cotton candy. Dugan was before my time.
But the others I have seen and remember. The decision on
who was the best is easy, easier than for any other position. I can never be convinced that anyone in this millennium has played third better than Brooks Robinson.
Needless to say, I don't hold this opinion in isolation. In a
brilliant sixteen-year career, Brooks simply rewrote the

book on third-base play. He wasn't fast, he didn't have a cannon arm; but he may have had the finest "nose" for the ball of any infielder in history, and his hands were as soft as a safecracker's. I can't believe that we will see his like again.

Yes, Wade, you're so right. Third base invites glamour, it breeds the stuff. I am reminded of a play by the great George Kell back in 1948 that illustrates the bravura style most of us associate with the hot corner. Playing with a recently healed broken wrist and on congenitally bad knees, Kell had his jaw shattered by a 150-mph drive from the bat of Joe DiMaggio. Reeling with pain and shock, Kell's first thought was to recover the ball and crawl to the base to make the force out. Only then did he permit himself the luxury of passing out in the fashion of normal humans. Believe me, third basemen don't eat quiche.

SEVEN
Keepers of the Keystone Sack

"Honus Wagner was the only shortstop in history who could tie his shoelaces without bending over."

—LEFTY GOMEZ

BASEBALL WRITING IS NOTORIOUS FOR ITS soggy fen of clichés and tired metaphors. But somewhere in the haze of a forgotten summer afternoon, a shirt-sleeved, arm-gartered journeyman in the press box was touched with genius. He called second base the keystone sack. If you could turn a baseball field on edge and rest it on the point of home plate, the appropriateness of the figure in spatial terms is immediately apparent. But the meaning goes deeper than that.

A large share of baseball's most intense action seems to

focus at or around second base. Maybe that's why it was recognized early in the development of the game that the base ought to have two guardians. And busy ones they have turned out to be.

When a runner reaches first base it is rarely cause for more than conventional stirring on the field or in the stands—unless, of course, he's a Rickey Henderson or a Tim Raines. But let him once reach second, be he the league's prize lead-foot, and fans move forward in their seats. Now things are happening. The runner is in "scoring position." It doesn't take an extra-base hit to bring him home. In a few instances, in fact, runners have been known to score from second on a fly ball.

On the field, shortstops, pitchers, and catchers begin to think pick-off. The defensive alignment shifts to fit the situation. Outfielders mentally flex their throwing arms. Once a base runner stands on second, he is a palpable threat to affect the outcome of the game. What goes on at second base is often the key to either victory or defeat.

Unlike the other positions, second base and shortstop rarely generate funny stories. We chuckle over the fielding gaucheries of Zeke Bonura at first or Pepper Martin at third. But move Zeke to second or Pepper to short and be assured that the laughter would stop abruptly. Out there in the center of the diamond, matters are deadly serious. Championships may be won or lost there. The middle infielders may handle between 70 and 75 percent of a team's season total of chances, including most of the toughest assists. It's baseball's version of trench warfare.

Every fan must be familiar with the principle that to win championships a team must be strong up the middle. Not infrequently teams have muddled through to victory with a so-so catcher who is a big hitter or a power-hitting center fielder of limited range. Few pennants have gone to teams that lacked a solid second-base combination. More than one general manager has learned to his sorrow what can happen if you seriously compromise on defensive strength in the middle of the diamond.

In 1950, having recently won with the aid of a fine defensive infield what was only the second pennant in the club's history, the Boston Braves traded shortstop Alvin Dark and second baseman Ed Stanky to the New York Giants for a couple of heavy-hitting but slow outfielders. Bill Veeck once characterized it as the worst trade in baseball history. The Giants' double-play totals soared, and in two seasons they moved from the second division to first place. The Braves' front office, in effect, had shipped the pennant to New York.

On the whole, today's general managers seem to me to be more sensitive to the absolute need for reliable gloves at the middle-infield positions, even to the extent of carrying a .190 hitter now and then. It may be that in an era that is producing young shortstops like Alan Trammell, Cal Ripken, Jr., Robin Yount, and Dickie Thon, as well as second basemen like Ryne Sandberg, Lou Whitaker, Johnny Ray, Tom Herr, and Bill Doran, the classic sacrifice of hitting for stronger defense in the middle may become a problem that GMs no longer have to face.

The idea of plugging the middle of the diamond with the surest hands available must go back a long way. When Harry Wright, baseball's first professional manager, was lured from Cincinnati to Boston in 1871 to head the city's entry in the newly formed National Association, he wisely installed his brother George at short and the equally gifted Ross Barnes at second. He was taking no chances on a leaky infield. It was a major reason for his Red Stockings capturing four straight championships, and the lesson can't have been lost on the other clubs. I suspect that there has been no period in the history of the game without its share of outstanding performers in the middle infield.

In the years that I have been watching baseball, the only change I can point to in play around second base is what appears to be greater consistency of performance among middle infielders of the past twenty to twenty-five years. Those gloves again? Maybe the Astroturf? I don't know. But I do know that it's uncanny for shortstops and second basemen to go for months without making an error. You begin to wonder if they are doing it with mirrors. I am thinking of players like Larry Bowa, Ozzie Smith, Bobby Grich, Joe Morgan, Rich Dauer, Manny Trillo, Frank White. But there are others as well. In 1973, Baltimore's second baseman, Bobby Grich, fielded .995 in 162 games while accepting more than 900 chances and turning 130 double plays. Good heavens, that's a star-first-baseman's average.

I can assure you that in the old days it was considered perfectly normal for the gifted shortstop or second baseman to be dazzling in the field one day and all thumbs the next. He was said to be having a bad day, and the team simply absorbed the damage. It reminds me of something that Arnold Hano told me about the Giants' great Travis Jackson, one of his favorite shortstops. "He was a brilliant and inconsistent fielder," Hano said. "He would let ground balls go right through his legs and then make the damndest play you ever saw in the hole. I've never seen a shortstop with an arm like that since."

Look at the shortstops, acknowledged to be the busier of the keystone pair and required to make the longest throw in the infield. In 1972, the Phillies' Larry Bowa confirmed the advantages of playing on artificial surface by making only nine misplays on more than seven hundred chances at Philadelphia's brand-new Veterans Stadium. In the same season, Detroit's Ed Brinkman shaved two off Larry's total while playing exclusively on grass and handling more chances.

I can't help contrasting these performances with Hall of Fame shortstop Luke Appling's 55 errors for the White Sox in 1933, or Hall of Famer Joe Cronin's 62 for Washington in 1929, or Hall of Famer Travis Jackson's 58 for the Giants in 1924, or Hall of Famer Joe Sewell's 59 for Cleveland in 1923, or Hall of Famer Dave Bancroft's 62 for the Giants in 1922. And if that doesn't strike you as exactly Cooperstown level fielding, measure it against non-Hall of Famer Johnny Gochnaur's blood-congealing 98 bobbles in just 134 games for Cleveland in 1903. I suspect that something may have changed besides the gloves and grass. Concentration maybe?

One thing I feel sure hasn't changed through the years is the characteristics that clubs are looking for when they scout a prospect for the middle infield. "Soft hands and agility" is the way Red Sox scout Earl Johnson responded to the question. "Quickness. And after that a strong and accurate arm, with the candidate for short needing the stronger arm." I doubt that any other scout's prescription will vary widely from this. Any baseball manual will tell you that at every position the first step is the most important. It will tell you further that at second and short the first step is critical. An outfielder caught leaning the wrong way can sometimes outrun his mistake. For an infielder, especially a middle infielder, it is next to impossible. Harry Wright, Al Spalding, and other pioneer managers may not have called it getting a jump on the ball, but I'll bet that's what they were looking for when they scouted a shortstop.

Given sure hands, range, a strong arm, and, if possible,

a healthy bat, what often determines whether a young player will make it to the majors as a middle infielder is his ability to make the double play. With many clubs this skill has probably been the litmus test for an aspiring second baseman, since he has the more difficult pivot.

I asked Bill Mazeroski, who in the 1950s and 1960s at Pittsburgh turned more double plays than any second baseman in history, if there was a special secret to mastering the play. "No, not really," he said. "You find somebody who knows how to do it and you work with him. It's technique first and then practice. If you don't have the right technique, you can practice all you want and you'll never get real good at it."

Mazeroski, who teamed principally with shortstops Dick Groat and Gene Alley in running up his league-leading totals, added that the only thing the second baseman needs to agree on with his partner is where he wants the ball thrown, "in front of the bag, over the bag, or behind the bag." The truth is that my romantic nature would have been better served had Maz told me that there was an arcane formula for turning the double play, one which he was honor bound not to share. I know that it would have made me feel less guilty about all those runners I missed at first.

It constitutes a tribute to this demanding play that the names of many of the great double-play combinations from the past are remembered with some of the same veneration we customarily lavish on fence-busting batting orders. You can still read admiring accounts of the slickness of such pioneer pairs as Chicago's Ned Williamson and Fred Pfeffer, who dazzled fans and frustrated opponents at West Side Park in the 1880s. In fact, it looks as though Williamson to Pfeffer to Anson was a lot better double-play combination than Tinker to Evers to Chance. But it didn't scan for newspaper doggerel, and so of the earlier three only Anson made it to the Hall of Fame—with his bat.

In the 1930s, the older fans of Boston were still singing the praises of the champion Beaneaters' keystone combination of Herman Long and Bobby Lowe when Joe Cronin teamed up with Bobby Doerr to succor the long-suffering Red Sox pitchers. For years in Cleveland you would not find a dissenting voice on the proposition that Terry Turner and Napoleon Lajoie were the classiest double-play artists ever to team up, albeit for a chronic loser of the early 1900s. Then Lou Boudreau and Joe Gordon got together to lead Cleveland to a world championship in the late 1940s, and confronted Indians fans with a dilemma. And in Philadelphia, the Athletics' Jack Barry and Eddie Collins, two of the earliest college graduates to play professional baseball, will be long remembered as young men who seemed to inject a touch of science into the task of getting two outs on one pitch.

Picture the generations of former pitchers fishing, playing golf, or just dozing in the Florida sun, who in large measure owed their comfortable retirement to the zeal and agility of double-play combinations like the Giants' Art Fletcher and Larry Doyle, Cincinnati's Horace Ford and Hughie Critz, the Cubs' Billy Jurges and Billy Herman, the Cardinals' Leo Durocher and Frankie Frisch, Detroit's Bill Rogell and Charlie Gehringer, the Yankees' Phil Rizzuto and Joe Gordon or Snuffy Stirnweiss or Jerry Coleman or Bobby Richardson (the "Scooter" fed them all), the Cardinals' Marty Marion and Red Schoendienst, Brooklyn's Pee Wee Reese and Jackie Robinson, the White Sox's Luis Aparicio and Nellie Fox, Baltimore's Mark Belanger and Bobby Grich, Cincinnati's Dave Concepcion and Joe Morgan, Kansas City's Freddie Patek and

Cookie Rojas, Philadelphia's Larry Bowa and Dave Cash. And there may be an equal number of great combinations that I can't dredge up. Detroit's Johnny Lipon and Jerry Priddy come suddenly to mind. Anyway, it helps you to understand why there have been so many twenty-game winners through the years.

I think that my favorite double-play combination was Reese and Robinson with the old Dodgers, not alone for their quickness of execution—and they showed that, certainly—but also for their buccaneer style around the bag. Any base runner with notions of breaking up a double play by intimidating this pair was indulging in fantasy. Robinson was as unyielding as a convent librarian. And Pee Wee, nowhere near as small as his nickname implies, was both tough and nimble. What a runner had to be most concerned about was the possibility of taking a 90-mph relay in the chop.

Speaking of Brooklyn and double plays, there is a tradition that baseball's first double play was started by Dickey Pearce, the five-feet-three-inch shortstop of the legendary Brooklyn Atlantics, sometime in the scantily documented 1860s. According to the standard account of the episode, Pearce trapped a pop fly in the infield, forced the dumbfounded base runner, and then threw out the batter. Leave it to a Brooklyn lad to stumble on a bargain, even on the ball field. How Dickey's new maneuver must have surprised and delighted the Flatbush Faithful, even as it confounded the opposition. He probably cut short a twenty-run inning. One of the most highly regarded players of his era, the resourceful Pearce is also credited with the invention of the bunt.

In view of the prestige of the Atlantics in the early days, it may be that Pearce, along with George Wright, his junior by eleven years, had considerable influence on

how shortstop came to be played by later generations. It
is a curious position, faintly anomalous in an otherwise
symmetrical arrangement of bases and players. In one of
his books, Henry Chadwick reveals that originally the
shortstop was looked upon as a supernumerary, a roving
fielder, free to assist any of the basemen as the spirit
moved him and the situation dictated. With an opponent
at bat, Chadwick reports, the shortstop generally took up
a neutral position somewhere between the pitcher and
second base. From that point he could move quickly to
where the action was, even into the outfield. Maybe shortstop was created when Alex Cartwright and his Knicker-
bockers reached New Jersey one Sunday afternoon and
discovered that they had an extra player for the day.
Chances are we will never know.

However the position evolved, it couldn't have taken a
genius to recognize that in a world dominated by right-
handed batters, a lot of base hits were going to bounce
through the left side of the infield. We don't know, of
course, exactly when the shortstop was dispatched to plug
the hole. However, baseball prints and other illustrations
from the early 1860s, which show the three basemen still
clinging to their bases with proprietary fervor, have the
shortstop already fixed in his present position. I have not
been able to discover when second basemen first began to
venture into the hole between second and first, although
that information may exist. My guess would be the early
1870s. Common sense (plus an increase in left-handed batters) had to encourage the idea of the shortstop's sharing
responsibility for the bag.

Although information on Dickey Pearce's play is
sketchy, we know quite a lot about George Wright and his
successors at shortstop. It's a measure of the relative
youth of baseball that Wright, the game's first full-time

professional shortstop, lived to attend the 1936 All-Star Game at Boston's Braves Field. He watched the National League's Leo Durocher and the American League's Luke Appling—both still with us, God be praised—play errorless ball. Is it possible that former National Leaguer Wright advised "the Lip" where to position himself against the power-laden American League lineup? In any case, the Nationals won their first All-Star Game ever, 4–3.

Clearly, a proper chronicle of shortstopping calls for a book in itself. Here it is only possible to acknowledge a few of the greatest performers at this very demanding position. When Wright retired at the end of the 1870s to become a manufacturer of sporting goods, young Jack Glasscock of Cleveland soon became known as "King of the Shortstops." Seldom has a newspaper sobriquet been so richly deserved. Contemporaries wrote admiringly of his great range and sure, soft hands. Glasscock, who was to play seventeen National League seasons, divided principally among Cleveland, St. Louis, and New York, led the league in fielding average six times, and his season highs for double plays, putouts, and assists stood unchallenged for years. Baseball historian William Akin writes of Glasscock that "he dominated his position more completely than any National Leaguer of the period." And he could hit, too.

Among Glasscock's contemporaries, Buffalo's Davy Force was one of the best. When Glasscock did not lead the league in fielding percentage, it was usually Force who did. And in the American Association, Bill Gleason, shortstop for the powerful St. Louis Browns, seems to have had no rival for class at the position.

In the 1890s, Boston's hard working Herman Long became an idol among Hub baseball fans. There's little doubt that Long was an aggressive fielder. He still holds the major-league lifetime record for average chances per game by a shortstop. However, Herman was something less than sure-handed. He has the unenviable distinction of having been charged with more errors—well over a thousand—than any man who has ever played the game. At Larry Bowa's normal rate of misplays, it would take him eighty-five years to tie Long's mark.

Bobby Wallace, the first American League shortstop to be elected to the Hall of Fame, must have been an early-day Phil Rizzuto. When the teenaged Bobby showed up for his first professional tryout at Pittsburgh in the 1880s, as shrewd a judge of talent as Connie Mack told him that he was too small to play and sent him packing, just as forty years later young Scooter would be chased from an Ebbets Field tryout by Casey Stengel. Like Rizzuto, Wallace persevered and eventually made it to the majors. In fact, toward the end of Wallace's twenty-five-year career, spent mostly with the St. Louis Browns, American League batters feared that Bobby might never retire. Wallace is credited with being the first shortstop to field a grounder and throw in one motion. The novel move must have helped him cut down thousands of base runners by a fraction of a step, and it quickly became a part of every shortstop's style.

In the twentieth century, most discussions of shortstop play begin and end with an evocation of the name of John "Honus" Wagner, called by John McGraw and other veteran observers of the game the greatest baseball player who ever lived. I have never talked with anyone who watched Honus play in his prime—and, sadly, there are but few still with us—who was willing to concede that "the Flying Dutchman" would be less than a superstar in any era. It seems evident that, like Babe Ruth and possibly one or two others, Ty

Cobb perhaps, Wagner's vast talents transcended the limitations imposed by the game in his day.

Wagner gave new meaning to range at shortstop. He was all over the left side of the infield and did not scruple to invade the right side if that's where a grounder was headed. Wherever the ball was hit, Honus seemed able to get in front of it and envelop it in his enormous hands. The story persists that so determined was Honus never to let a ball slip from his grasp that he would sometimes come up with a sampling of infield dirt and grass as well. My father swore that it was true.

As a youth, Wagner was ungainly in appearance. Never have externals been such a poor index to an athlete's ability. Still, it may explain why Honus was in his fifth full season in the National League and had been played at a half dozen positions before it dawned on as able a manager as Fred Clarke that the Dutchman was a born shortstop.

I got to talk with Honus once when I was a kid and he was still active as a kind of honorary coach with the Pirates, suiting up dutifully for every game, a slightly bent but still sturdy figure with spiky gray hair. He autographed a scorecard for me. "John Honus Wagner," he wrote. I don't recall the substance of our two-minute conversation. I could have asked him what it was like to bat against Christy Mathewson or to steal second against Jimmy Archer or to rob Ty Cobb of a base hit up the middle in a World Series. I know that I asked none of these because I would have remembered the answers. Most likely I said something like, "Well, how's it goin' today, Honus?" Young fool, I.

It looks like shortstopping after the Age of Wagner may have suffered a bit of a decline. The souped-up ball could have had something to do with it. It can't have been an easy or enviable job to have to learn how to scoop up those white lightning bolts. Honus never had to contend with the problem because the rabbit in the ball did not become fully grown until 1920. This is not to say that there were no good shortstops around. Jack Barry and Art Fletcher were pretty good. The Yankees' Roger Peckinpaugh, the Red Sox's Everett Scott, and the Braves' Rabbit Maranville were not only good, but long-lived. Maranville played twenty-three seasons. In fact, Rabbit must have had a superglove. Way back in 1954, he made it into the Hall of Fame with a .258 lifetime batting average. He was a colorful infielder and always a favorite with the press. Perhaps his reputation for being good copy eased his way to Cooperstown. Maranville was noted for catching pop flies against his chest, a style that Willie Mays would later raise to new heights of celebrity in the outfield.

The shortstop trade between World War I and World War II? Well, you must first understand that in those days everyone was expected to swing the bat with gusto—shortstops, pitchers, bullpen catchers—everyone. If you didn't, you might soon find yourself assessing boardinghouse accommodations in a Three I League city. Bancroft and Jackson in New York, Glenn Wright and later Arky Vaughan in Pittsburgh, the Yankees' Mark Koenig, Washington's Joe Cronin, Cleveland's Joe Sewell, the White Sox's Luke Appling, the Cubs' Woody English, the Browns' Red Kress, Detroit's Bill Rogell, the Car-dinals' Charley Gelbert, the Phillies' Dick Bartell—all these clipped the ball as well as the average outfielder does today. And they were the good fielders of their day, too. Granted, we're not talking about Ozzie Smith or Luis Aparicio standards. But over the course of a season they could get the job done. And they knew that they were reasonably secure so long as they kept swatting the ball.

During a four-year stretch at the height of his career in the 1930s, Leo Durocher averaged .270 at the plate and drove in about 65 runs a year, pretty good by today's standards. His reward was to be hailed universally as "the All-American Out." We kids assumed that it was only Leo's reputation for sporting the slickest glove in the league that was delaying his ticket to Sioux City. And we may have been correct.

It is possible that social conditions in America played a role in the quality of shortstopping during the Depression. Bear in mind that jogging and aerobics were still forty years in the future. Beer was ten cents a glass, in some places a nickel, and a four-course steak dinner could be had for a buck and a half—if you had that kind of money. Ballplayers did. They also had big appetites. After a few seasons of collecting meal money from the club's traveling secretary, shortstops may have begun to feel as if the distance between second and third had been widened to 150 feet. On the bright side, that extra bulk must have come in handy for belting the ball off the fences.

Take the case of the late American League chairman Joe Cronin. It was said that when Joe arrived in Washington from Kansas City he had a lean body, a square jaw, and an iron glove. But after a few seasons the young shortstop got accustomed to the middle of the diamond and became one of the best. The trouble was that at about the same time he also got accustomed to the salary of a playing manager, and no longer even had to look at the prices on the menu when he took Mrs. Cronin out to dinner at Washington's fanciest restaurants. On top of that, Mrs. Cronin was probably a super cook. Let it be said, though, that at any weight Joe was a grand guy and an exemplary player, manager, and baseball executive. He will be missed.

Leo Durocher may have been eating as much as anyone else, but he was known to be an avid ballroom dancer and seemed able to keep his weight down. With the kind of bat he was swinging, the dancing probably saved his career.

For many years I have harbored the private notion that Dick Bartell may have been the most underrated shortstop of the period. Not long ago I was pleasantly surprised to have no less an authority than Charlie Gehringer volunteer a reinforcement of that judgment. "I played one year with Dick Bartell," Charlie said, "and I always thought he was probably one of the greatest shortstops. I played with him in the World Series in 1940 and we were both over the hill then. But he was tremendous even at that age."

It seems to me that in the early 1940s, baseball experienced something like a shortstop renaissance, not unlike the one we are seeing now. Perhaps it was so striking because there was no comparable surge in defensive skill at the other positions, at least as far as I can determine. In any case, in the space of a couple of seasons, Lou Boudreau, Pee Wee Reese, Marty Marion, Phil Rizzuto, the Braves' Eddie Miller, and Cincinnati's Eddie Joost all arrived in the majors. Soon pitchers were smiling and leg-hitters were sulking. These were young infielders of extraordinary quickness and range, and they helped establish a new standard for the position that was to carry well into the post-war period.

In some respects Boudreau was the most gifted of the group. For eight of his first nine seasons he led the American League in fielding percentage and rarely ever fell below one hundred double plays a year. Not endowed with great speed, Lou made up for it with his quick start, and more than that with his extraordinary ability to read the hitters. Today, with widespread use of form charts and even computers, positioning fielders against specific batters is not far from routine. In the early 1940s, apparently, it was a matter of individual initiative and much less common. In the mid-1950s Pee Wee Reese told Tom Meany, "This position play was comparatively rare when I broke in."

In 1946, Boudreau, then Cleveland's playing manager, carried his analysis of hitters to new levels when he ordered his entire infield to position themselves to the right of second base against Ted Williams. All Ted had to do was push three or four hits a game through the gaping hole on the left side and that might have been the end of what was called the Boudreau Shift. Lou's strategy, however, was as much keyed to Williams's tempestuous personality as it was to his batting habits. Ted stubbornly insisted upon trying to pull the ball over everyone's head and the shift had the desired effect. Williams's run production against the Indians dropped appreciably. Today, modified shifts against dead pull hitters are almost commonplace.

With the arrival in 1950 at Chicago's Comiskey Park of Venezuelan Chico Carrasquel, a new element entered the shortstopping trade—the Latin touch. It's probably romantic nonsense to suggest that Carrasquel and the Latin-American shortstops who followed him in the next dozen years—Aparicio, Leo Cardenas, Willie Miranda, Chico Fernandez, Jose Valdivielso, Ruben Amaro, Jose Pagan and Zoilo Versalles—introduced the panache of the matador to the middle infield. But the idea is seductive.

Paul Richards, Carrasquel's first major-league manager, doesn't dismiss the notion out of hand, but he sees it in distinctly analytical terms. "Chico was a tall boy," Richards says, "and maybe that made it look as if he were a little different. He used a lot of instinct to get a jump on the ball. The fact of the matter is that Chico had that knack or ability that Brooks Robinson had of getting his glove open quickly, long before the ball got to him. And it seemed always to go right into his glove."

For all their dashing style of play, not every Latin-American shortstop scaled the heights of Carrasquel, Aparicio, Versalles, Campaneris, and Concepcion. There was, for example, Elio Chacon. On second thought, Elio did achieve a kind of immortality. He played for the 1962 Mets.

While this Latin-American revolution was in progress, a number of shortstops cast in a more reserved, Anglo-Saxon mold—Cincinnati's Roy McMillan, Milwaukee's Johnny Logan, Washington's Ed Brinkman, Pittsburgh's Dick Groat, the Cardinals' Dal Maxvill—were also building long and honorable careers in the center of the diamond. And let's not forget Ernie Banks, who, while no match for his crosstown counterpart Carrasquel in pyrotechnics with the glove, was still no slouch going into the hole, all the while poling some forty-plus home runs a season. Never before or since has such thunder been heard from the bat of a shortstop.

Demands on the shortstop have probably been so high for so long that most of the truly significant developments came early in the history of the game. Changes in style seem fewer and less frequent than for other positions. Pee Wee Reese, who played more than two thousand games at short and may have seen another thousand since, believes that what few changes he has seen since he broke in can be traced to artificial surfaces and improved gloves. "When you have Astroturf you can play a lot deeper," he says. "I think Astroturf can make an excellent fielder out of an ordinary fielder." The only clearly identifiable change he notes in play at the position is Dave Concepcion's bounce throw to first on the artificial surface, which he thinks makes good sense because it obviates an overthrow of first base on a quick-release play. In its essentials, though, Pee Wee sees shortstop being played the way it was when he first pulled on a glove. "Not a lot has changed as far as I can see," he says. "You have to make the double play by crossing the bag the same way. You have to stay down. And you have to catch the ball out in front of you."

As far back as I can remember, it has been assumed among fans and amateur players that second base is a lot easier to play than short. I wonder to what extent this folk conviction is supported by the experience of 116 years of professional baseball. Obviously, the second baseman has a shorter throw. And there are fewer left-handed batters. But there is still a lot to do out there—running clumsy first basemen off balls hit far to your left, for example, and avoiding homicidal base runners on the double play. It's not a cakewalk.

A corollary notion I have read for years is that a young, fast shortstop will permit a team to carry an older, slower second baseman who has a potent bat. I haven't taken the time to pin down a general manager on that one. And does it work in reverse? Does the acquisition of a Ryne Sandberg or a Julio Cruz permit you to carry an Arky Vaughan or a "Junior" Stephens for a couple of extra seasons?

One thing that the history of the game does appear to demonstrate is that second basemen, even those who are top fielders, can hit better than shortstops. Don't ask me why this should be so. Look at the list of second basemen who are lifetime .300 hitters and you find names like Lajoie, Cupid Childs, Eddie Collins, Gehringer, Hornsby, Frisch, Robinson, Herman, and Buddy Myer. These are solid to superb gloves, and with the exception of Hornsby probably never yielded a step to a shortstop in their careers. On the list of shortstops who batted .300 lifetime you find Vaughan, Cecil Travis, Sewell, Appling, Cronin, Johnny Pesky, Harvey Kuenn, and Ed McKean—all-right guys, to be sure, but not names likely to cause Ozzie Smith any loss of sleep.

It looks like the tradition of the stronger bat at second may have begun right at the start with the elegant Ross Barnes of the Chicago White Stockings, the major leagues' first .400 hitter and one of the greatest fielders of his generation. Barnes had earlier served an apprenticeship alongside George Wright at Boston in the National Association. In the five seasons they played together, Barnes outhit Wright by twenty-six percentage points, no mean feat. Ross also hit the major leagues' first home run.

The other nineteenth-century second basemen whose names come up most frequently in historical studies that touch on fielding are Fred "Sure Shot" Dunlap, who broke in with Cleveland but seemed to move to a new club every couple of seasons; John "Bid" McPhee, who spent his entire eighteen-year career in Cincinnati but switched leagues midway; and Chicago's Fred Pfeffer, known to the city's large and admiring German population as "Unser Fritz." In what appears to be the grand tradition of Gold Glove quality second basemen, all were good hitters. Dunlap even had one .400 season.

It is said that Dunlap, who scorned gloves to the very end of his career, could throw equally well with either hand. It's too bad that scorers didn't think to record how many runners he cut down at second and third with quick left-handed throws. Dunlap is reported to have been illiterate as well as ambidextrous. If so, he never let it shake his self-esteem. He is known to have put his "X" on some of the fattest contracts of his time.

The bilingual Pfeffer may not have been as shrewd as Dunlap about money matters, but he was sufficiently literate to have written books on baseball after his retirement. Since he played next to Cap Anson, Fritz had little trouble keeping his weight down and his range up. He became one of the earliest masters of the double play.

Although Bid McPhee did not begin to use a glove until late in his career, he may have been the most effective second baseman of his century. When he retired in 1899, having played more than 2,100 games at the position, Bid held the major-league season *and* lifetime records for fielding average, putouts, assists, and double plays. That's hard to argue against.

Just as Honus Wagner was to rewrite the book for shortstops in the new century, Napoleon Lajoie established standards of excellence for the second basemen who followed him. Those who watched him play say that despite his size (a bit over two hundred pounds) he was the most graceful infielder of his time, especially when turning the double play.

For all Lajoie's gifts, the man whose name most often shows up at second base on all-time teams in the first half of this century is Eddie Collins. In terms of durability in the field, at the plate, and on the base paths, Collins appears to have been an early-day Joe Morgan. Eddie played a record 2,601 games at second in twenty-five different seasons, a mark that Morgan will fall just short of if he holds to his retirement announcement. Collins first achieved fame as a member of a Philadelphia Athletics infield that manager (and owner) Connie Mack said he would not sell for $100,000. Don't laugh. You could buy a franchise for that kind of money in those days.

When I was a kid I used to play second base occasionally on a beautifully maintained field in the little town of Millerton, New York, Eddie Collins's birthplace. Imagining that I was standing on the very spot where the fabulous Eddie had picked up the rudiments of fielding, I was stirred to hurl myself in front of ground balls I would surely have given up on back on my home field in Kissena Park. Years later, when the bruised elbows and lacerated forearms had long since healed, I learned to my chagrin that Collins had never played anything but shortstop before Mack shifted him to second base in 1909. Anyway, I got to stand in the same batter's box, unless Eddie perversely grew up as a right-handed batter.

Along with Lajoie and Collins, the second basemen you are most likely to read of from the period before 1920 are Pittsburgh's Claude Ritchey, Brooklyn's George Cutshaw, the Cubs' Johnny Evers, the Yankees' Jimmy Williams, the Browns' Del Pratt, and Cincinnati's Miller Huggins, who made the Hall of Fame for his managing rather than his ability to turn the double play (which was not bad). Apparently, none was in a class with Lajoie and Collins, but they were all competent, if we can trust the record, and most were handy with the bat, particularly Pratt.

Whenever possible I like to check with fans old enough to have seen some of the great fielders of the early part of the century to test whether their accounts will support or refute the record book. With this in mind I telephoned my uncle, who is eighty and lives in upstate New York, to seek his estimate of some of the second basemen of the 1920s and 1930s. He is an ardent Mets fan and has long been a sound judge of baseball flesh. For example, he prophesied before I could shave that my baseball career would peak out in Summer Recreation League. The only reason I ever hesitate to consult my uncle is that he is inclined to give excessive weight to hitting—very much a disciple of ash—and he has a McGraw-like impatience with what modern players call "life-style problems."

"Second base, eh?" my uncle said pleasantly. "I don't know where you would find a better pair of hands than on little Hughie Critz. Cincinnati, later went to the Giants. Slick as a greased eel around the bag. Good double-play man. Couldn't hit his hat size, though."

"Two-six-eight lifetime, Uncle. Not bad for a middle infielder. Exactly the same as Joe Gordon, in fact—without the homers, of course."

My uncle snorted. "As I said, Hughie couldn't hit for sour apples. Oscar Melillo same thing. Little bandy-legged fella—with the Browns. Oscar claimed he trained on spaghetti—like Tom Lasorda. I guess Oscar didn't digest it as well. Hundred and forty pounds with uniform and spikes. Lightning on the double play."

"I suppose then that Hornsby was more to your taste at second. Or Frisch."

My uncle's voice sounded more enthusiastic. "Understand, Rajah was no Eddie Collins. But you didn't have to worry about anything going between his legs. That wasn't true of everybody, you know."

"Tell me about Frisch—and Collins."

"Oh, my, the old Fordham Flash. What Frankie wouldn't do to win a ball game. Throw himself on a ground ball like it was a live grenade and he was trying to save the shortstop's life. And come up throwing."

"Collins?"

"Of course Eddie had slowed down some when I first saw him. Still smooth as egg custard. Always thinking ahead. Made every chance look easy—like Gehringer."

"I saw a lot of Charlie when I was a kid. He was a picture in the field and at bat. I'll bet you like Billy Herman, too."

"Best hit-and-run man in the business."

"Glove?"

"Good. Very good. Ground ball had to be trailing smoke to get by Billy."

"I don't suppose you approved of Max Bishop with his two-seventy-four lifetime."

My uncle chuckled. "Didn't know he hit that well. I would have guessed two-fifty tops. Connie Mack's lead-off man. Couldn't hit, but he walked more than Babe Ruth. Like Eddie Yost. I don't know why Mack had him leading off. I don't think Max stole a base in his life."

"I want to talk about fielding, Uncle."

"Well, Max was all right. Precise little guy. Like Bobby Richardson. Good snap throw, too."

"What about Bucky Harris? He only had a two-seventy-four lifetime average and he made the Hall of Fame. He must have been a super fielder."

"Nothing spectacular. He got the job done. He must have made Cooperstown on his ability to manage Goose Goslin. I'll say this, he and Peckinpaugh could make that double play faster than you could watch."

"Peckinpaugh. I read that he made eight errors in the 1925 World Series, several on perfect double-play balls. Eight errors. Don't you think, Uncle, that great as some of the old-timers were, this sort of thing proves the superiority of the modern player?" It was a mistake. I knew it before the words were out.

"Are you paying long-distance rates just to insult my intelligence?" my uncle roared. "Never in the course of human history has there been such a collection of spoiled, avaricious, self-indulgent, egomaniacal. . . . Imagine demanding a million a year for hitting one-ninety and fielding nine hundred. Taking money for posing in their underwear. Doing time and not hitting their cell numbers when they get out—at a million a year . . ."

"Wait a minute, Uncle, please. No personalities. Times

have changed. Different world, different game. Besides, I made this call to talk about fielding."

"Can't hit their cell numbers, I say. Probably had them locked in the bottom tier, too."

I hate to hang up on my uncle. But it happens sometimes.

In any case, since World War II I have seen some first-rate second-base play by men about whose life-styles I don't know a thing. The sports pages didn't cover players' investment portfolios and paternity suits until about ten years ago. There was the Red Sox's Bobby Doerr, who may not own a share of AT&T to this day. What a stone wall he was on the right side of the infield at Fenway. And he could hit well enough to please even my uncle. And what I wouldn't give to see the graceful Red Schoendienst again. Or the doughty Nellie Fox, his cheek distended by a monstrous chaw. Without checking I would be willing to bet that Nellie was never on the disabled list in his entire career. And yet he died young.

Who could forget Eddie Stanky, "the Brat," who did not hit but always seemed to be on base—or robbing someone else of a base hit. The energetic Bill Mazeroski, placid Bobby Richardson, Detroit's steady Frank Bolling. And more recently, Morgan, Grich, Rojas, Cash, Dauer, Trillo, White, Cruz—not to mention youngsters like Sandberg, Ray, Whitaker. We seem to get deeper in fine second basemen with each passing season.

On opening day in 1982, Phillies second baseman Manny Trillo was charged with an error on his first chance of the game. His otherwise good throw hit a base runner in the back. That was April 8. Trillo did not make another error until the last day of July, 90 games and 479 chances later. On that occasion he juggled a hard smash off the bat of the Cubs' Bill Buckner and failed to nip him at first. The call might have gone either way without raising protest. I estimate that Manny must have been hitting about .270 at the time. And he would hit no homers that season and drive in fewer than 40 runs.

When it became evident that Trillo's errorless streak had ended, more than fifty thousand people at Philadelphia's Veterans Stadium rose and applauded him for five minutes. It was the kind of tribute that in the past had been reserved exclusively for batting titans, like Babe Ruth, Ted Williams, and Hank Aaron.

Baseball fans, I think we have seen the millennium.

EIGHT
Paladins on the Picket Line

*"The first three qualities to look for in an out-
field candidate are speed, speed—and speed."*
—TRADITIONAL

UNLESS YOUR PITCHER HAS SUDDENLY LOST
three feet off his fastball, the outfield is not what you
would call a busy place. In the course of a season, a regular outfielder may be expected to handle an average of
just over two chances a game, with the center fielder having the highest figure. In fact, there are periods when a
right fielder can have more time on his hands than a Mos-
cow investment counselor. In 1926, for example, Baby
Doll Jacobson, newly arrived in Fenway Park's spacious
right field after an outstanding career with the Browns,

played seven consecutive games for the Red Sox without a putout or an assist. I doubt, in fact, whether statisticians even keep track of the times that an outfielder goes nine innings without a chance. It must run into the thousands.

Anyone who ever watched Moose Solters or the Cubs' "Mad Russian," Lou Novikoff, knows how all this idleness can generate problems in concentration for a healthy young man held at a distance from home plate. In the days when baseball was played in sunlight and on grass, the more service-oriented fielders often turned volunteer grounds keepers, passing the time between pitches by flattening offending anthills with their spikes, plucking dandelions, tossing away microscopic pebbles. For twenty-two years, Mel Ott kicked away with his right toe at something in the right-field grass at the Polo Grounds, but a generation of fans who inspected the area never could discover what it was. In any case, enemy base runners foolish enough to put Mel's concentration to the test by going from first to third almost always lost.

Under the circumstances it's not surprising that coaches routinely urge young outfielders to forget their stock portfolios for the moment and get up on their toes for each pitch. The fact is that however long his periods of inactivity, an outfielder may be called upon on short notice to perform any one of a multitude of chores—backing up the man on his flank, fielding grounders, playing a carom off the wall, backing up one or more bases, throwing to the correct base, hitting the cutoff man, running to the infield to help in a rundown, throwing to the plate, and so on. And overriding these is his responsibility to deal consistently with that crowning enigma of baseball, the fly ball. When he's not swinging a bat, an outfielder is above all else a flycatcher.

Traditionally, catching a fly ball has been viewed as the

easiest play in the game. Why, then, after almost a century and a half of baseball experience, should there be a shadow of uncertainty about mastering the art? Because, say the physicists, who take an occasional breather from quantum theory to probe such trivia, we're still not quite sure how it is done. "One of the unique aspects of the skill," Professor Peter Brancazio of Brooklyn College reported to a professional meeting in 1983, "is that there is no way to verbalize it or to teach someone else how to do it. [Catching flies], it seems, must be completely self-taught at a non-verbal level." Let me add to the professor's scientific observation the pragmatic view that anyone who has ever camped under one of the treacherous things knows in his heart that he should never bet his life—or even the family car—on the catch.

Martin Quigley tells a story that may offer high-school ball hawks food for thought. On a business trip to New York many years ago, Quigley took in a baseball game at Yankee Stadium. In the course of the afternoon, someone lofted a lazy fly ball to Joe DiMaggio for which the Yankee Clipper did not have to move a step. "Joe raised his hands," Quigley relates, "and the ball hit his glove and fell to the ground." Awed silence enveloped the stadium. The greatest center fielder of his generation had dropped an easy fly. Still reeling in disbelief, Quigley left the ball park with the firm conviction that never again in his lifetime would he witness such an unlikely event.

Back home in St. Louis a week later, Quigley was at Sportsman's Park to see the Cardinals play. Early in the game someone hit a soft fly to Terry Moore, the National League's reigning center fielder and one of the greatest of all time. "Without moving from his tracks," Quigley says, "Terry raised his cupped hands, the ball hit the glove and fell to the ground." Quigley was ready to acknowledge that indeed nothing is certain but death and taxes and that even the tax collector may boot one from time to time.

For all the mystery that surrounds the fly ball, it is a fact that the modern big-league outfielder can be counted on to gather in between 98 and 99 out of every 100 he gets under, roughly 325 putouts a year for a full-time player. It's the "gets under" that can sometimes present problems. Lefty Gomez once said, perhaps half serious, "I owe my success as a pitcher to clean living and a fast outfield." Some outfielders can and do outrun their mistakes.

Yet speed isn't the whole answer to success on the plastic greensward. "An outfield candidate must have quickness so that he can range," Baltimore's director of player development and scouting, Tom Giordano, told me. "He can have all the speed in the world and if he can't get a jump on the ball, he's always going to be trying to catch up with it. Quickness is vitally important to us. Speed then comes in its proper second place."

And now it turns out that even quickness and speed may not in themselves be enough. Professor Brancazio theorizes that the pursuer of fly balls may profit from acute hearing as well. His research suggests that inner-ear sensors may play as big a part in judging fly balls as does vision. Among his observations is that a person following an object in flight, such as an outfielder setting up for a fly ball, moves his head as well as his eyes. "This coordination of sensory input with body motion," Brancazio reported last year, "evidently follows a neural pathway that has been established through the familiar behavioral process of learning through trial and error. . . . We may actually be judging fly balls by ear."

Is it possible that Babe Herman's real problem was excessive earwax?

We find support of a kind for Professor Brancazio's theory in the career of the St. Louis Browns' Curt Welch, acknowledged the most spectacular center fielder of the 1880s. It was widely reported at the time that Welch judged fly balls by the sound of the bat. And early in this century, George Burns, the Giants' legendary ball hawk, claimed that he, too, relied on the crack of the bat to tell him where the ball was headed. Burns said that based solely on the sound he could confidently turn his back on the ball and run to the spot where it would come down.

Baseball records tell us very little about the fly-catching skill of outfielders in the earliest days of the game, and it is probably just as well. We know from the early rules that there was trepidation about the fly ball. Until the outbreak of the Civil War the batter could be retired legally if his fly was caught on the first bounce. Baseball historian Robert Smith tells us that in the 1850s amateur teams would demonstrate their machismo by challenging opponents to play "the fly game," in which by agreement only a caught fly was out. Smith adds that in those days the fans screamed with delight whenever an outfielder did succeed in catching a high fly.

The Brooklyn Atlantics' Jack Chapman built a considerable reputation in the 1860s and 1870s as an outfielder who could deal consistently with flying baseballs. But no other names have come down to us. And as late as 1884, we find a full-time National League outfielder, Philadelphia's Jack Manning, posting a fielding average of only .847. When you consider that Manning played alongside the major leagues' premier ball hawk, Jim Fogarty, who made more putouts in the decade of the 1880s than did any other outfielder in the game, you can only conclude that Manning was a slow learner. But perhaps we shouldn't be too hard on Jack's performance. The league's top mark for the year was only .917, and the great Fogarty himself was two percentage points shy of that.

And then there was Cleveland's "Gentle Willie" Murphy. He fielded a neat .720 for forty-seven games in the same year. Yes, 1884 was Gentle Willie's only season in the bigtime.

In reviewing the play of pioneer outfielders we must bear in mind that some played without gloves. In addition, the quality of playing surfaces varied, and they often had to contend with a menace only eliminated from the game within the memory of living persons—crowd interference. As recently as 1922, Yankee center fielder Whitey Witt was knocked unconscious and hospitalized after being struck in the head by a pop bottle thrown from an overflow crowd in St. Louis. And way back at the beginning of things, fans of the Brooklyn Atlantics helped to end the historic two-year winning streak of the Cincinnati Red Stockings when they jumped on the back of Cincinnati right-fielder Cal McVey to delay his return of the ball to the infield on an eleventh-inning Brooklyn hit.

To be sure, crowds on or close to the playing field can sometimes be as helpful to the hometown outfielders as they are threatening to the visitors. In game eight of the 1912 World Series, Red Sox right fielder Harry Hooper robbed the Giants' Larry Doyle of a home run by throwing himself backward into the temporary bleachers at Fenway Park and letting the fans cradle his body while he made the catch. The editor of *Spalding's Guide* later wrote that the catch was palpably illegal. But the umpire allowed it and the play cost the Giants the game and the series.

With the advent of the large modern ball park and the concurrent elimination of overflow crowds, fan interference seems pretty much limited to someone reaching out to touch a ball that's in play. At least I rarely hear of things being thrown at visiting players. In the most benign assault on record, White Sox right fielder Al Smith was doused with a cup of beer during the 1959 World Series.

Construction of the first steel and concrete ball parks in the early part of the century helped solve the problem of having fans at the playing level, but they introduced a new menace to outfielders—the uneven duel with a concrete wall. Joe DiMaggio once commented grimly that the test of an outfielder's skill comes when he has to go against the fence to make a catch. Some outfielders have passed that test at the cost of their careers, notably Brooklyn's Pete Reiser, who was seriously injured several times in his fearless pursuit of the ball. In 1934, the Yankees' Hall of Fame center fielder Earle Combs had his career ended abruptly and almost lost his life when he fractured his skull in a collision with the wall in St. Louis. Partly because of the experience of Reiser, Combs, and others, the custom of padding the outfield walls or putting up flexible inner barriers is now virtually universal.

In the popular mind, the wooden barriers of eighty to a hundred years ago were thought to be less intimidating to outfielders. For many decades the story was circulated and believed that Bill Lange, Chicago's superb center fielder of the 1890s, once crashed right through a wooden fence to make a catch. Lange had the size to make such an exploit plausible, but inevitably some spoilsport young historian blew the story by exposing its lack of documentation. It tells something about Lange's reputation for courage and skill in the outfield that fans were willing to accept the story uncritically for almost half a century.

In an episode that is documented, Detroit's "Fat Bob" Fothergill shattered a wooden fence in pursuit of a fly ball during an exhibition game in Roanoke, Virginia, in the

1930s. Regrettably, the account fails to note whether Fothergill made the catch.

There's hardly a greater staple of the Hot Stove League than retelling stories of great catches in the outfield. It bears out what Charlie Gehringer observed about fans being more likely to remember outfield plays than those in the infield. Bring three or four vintage baseball fans together of a winter's evening, the refrigerator filled with beer and nothing better on television than basketball, hockey, or demolition derby, and chances are they will begin to regale one another with tales of acrobatic catches they have seen.

Frankly, I feel left out in such sessions. After all my years of watching baseball, I can't claim to have seen an outfield catch that could be called historic. Yes, I *was* watching television when Willie Mays made his catch against Vic Wertz in the 1954 World Series. And a dozen or more times I have seen on film Al Gionfriddo's do-or-die stab of Joe DiMaggio's colossal drive in the 1947 Series. But that really doesn't count. I have seen nothing like it at the ball park.

Arnold Hano, on the other hand, not only was present for Mays's catch, and built a fine book around it, but almost a quarter of a century earlier, he happened to be at the Polo Grounds to see the Giants' Hall of Fame third baseman Fred Lindstrom, when he was doing double duty as right fielder, go ten or twelve feet up the right-center-field wall at the 465-foot marker to rob Pittsburgh's Gus Suhr on what may have been the greatest catch ever made at a New York ball park. Hano is either luckier than I am or he goes to more games.

I assume that with the advent of sports television in the 1940s, all great catches in the outfield since World War II have been preserved on film or videotape. Allowing for some distortion by the medium, they can be reviewed and reevaluated at leisure by generations still unborn. What a boon to future baseball fans. Catches made before the age of electronic marvels must live solely in the descriptions of those who witnessed them—fans and baseball writers. Of course, that has its own charm.

Many times I have heard old-timers tell of a catch that Joe DiMaggio made against Hank Greenberg at Yankee Stadium in 1939. Joe, they say, caught up with the 450-foot line shot about a step from the monuments in center field (that's old Yankee Stadium, remember). Having seen Di-Mag make many a long drive look like a routine chance, I can easily credit the story. In fact, I can picture the play.

Joe may have aborted many triples in his day, but he had the tables turned on him more than once, especially in World Series games. Everyone knows about the Gion-friddo grab in 1947. But even in Joe's first World Series in 1936, Hank Leiber robbed him on a 460-foot poke into the bleacher well at the Polo Grounds. And in the 1942 Series against St. Louis, Terry Moore denied DiMag on what could have been the longest ball ever struck at Yankee Stadium that didn't leave the playing field. It went to the deepest corner of left center, possibly 485 feet from home plate. "It seemed like to me I ran a full minute before I caught up with the ball," Moore said, recounting the play not long ago. "I had my back to the infield, caught the ball over my shoulder, and then almost hit the fence."

There's probably some simple reason, which a psychologist could quickly pinpoint, that so many of the miraculous catches we read about were made in World Series games—Philadelphia's Rube Oldring's epic shoestring on the Giants' Moose McCormick in 1913, the Red Sox's Duffy Lewis on a home-run bid by Philadelphia's Gavvy Cravath in 1915, Sam Rice's swan dive into the temporary bleachers at Washington's Griffith Stadium to rob the Pirates' Earl Smith, Sandy Amoros's double-play catch on the Yankees' Yogi Berra to nail down Brooklyn's first world championship in 1955, Ron Swoboda's horizontal grab against Brooks Robinson (which helped produce the Mets' miracle in 1969), Joe Rudi's human-fly act in Cincinnati to rob Denis Menke of extra bases and speed Oakland on its way to three successive world titles, and perhaps many more that don't immediately come to mind.

Catches made during the season don't stick in the memory as well unless there's an additional fillip to them, like the seat-of-the-pants bare-handed grab by Terry Moore against Mel Ott in St. Louis in 1936, which may have been the first sliding basket catch, now a standard maneuver by outfielders. That one has held place in the fading memories of old-timers for almost fifty years.

When the subject of circus catches has been exhausted, outfield buffs often turn to stories of great throws, or rather great arms, since specific throws have a way of shifting about in the memory bank. Any old Brooklyn fan will assure you that Carl Furillo, one of the Boys of Summer, could have thrown a ball right through the back wall of Ebbets Field and out onto McKeever Place had he wanted to show off, but Carl knew that Branch Rickey would have promptly billed him for repairs. Closer to reality, Pee Wee Reese told me that throws from Furillo actually seemed to gain speed after they bounced.

One of the first great arms to gain the attention and respect of National League base runners belonged to Louis Sockalexis, Cleveland's giant Penobscot Indian right fielder, after whom, it is said, the team was eventually named. Far into the twentieth century there were writers and fans who insisted that "Big Sock" had the strongest throwing arm ever seen on a diamond.

One of Sockalexis's successors at Cleveland, "Shoeless

Joe" Jackson, was reputed to be able to throw more than 350 feet with ease and accuracy. In one of the first throwing contests on record during a benefit game at Fenway Park, Jackson outthrew all the prominent outfielders of his time, including Ruth, Speaker, and Cobb.

An interesting example of an ordinary outfielder who held on in the majors early in the century largely on the value of his unusually powerful arm is the Athletics' Bris Lord. In his eight-year career he only batted .256 and drove in a sprinkling of runs, so it's a cinch he had to have something else going for him.

You will probably get as many nominations for the title of Greatest Arm as the number of fans you talk with. In my childhood, the odds-on favorite among adults seemed to be the Yankees' Bob Meusel. There are still a few old fans around who assert that the equal of "Long Bob" has not yet come along the pike. The Cardinals' Chick Hafey was well respected in those days, too, as were the Athletics' Al Simmons and Cincinnati's Edd Roush. Roush, the oldest living member of the Hall of Fame, told me that throwing from the outfield became noticeably easier after the adoption of the lively ball, which was lighter in weight, and also after the ban on the spitball. Not only was the old ball heavier by nature and therefore harder to throw, Edd said, but it was often additionally weighted with moisture.

Mel Ott, Joe DiMaggio, and Terry Moore probably had the most feared arms of the 1930s and early 1940s. The Braves' Vince DiMaggio could really throw, too, as could his teammate Gene Moore. A left-handed thrower, Moore used to cut down squadrons of National League base runners every year, but somehow this intelligence never trickled through to the Giants' third-base coaches when Gene visited the Polo Grounds. If I had a dollar for every wayward Giant runner I watched him erase from the base paths, I could go to the ball game tonight and have enough left over for a scorecard.

What a pity Vince DiMaggio wasn't blessed with good vision. In addition to having a bazooka arm, he was fast and a marvelous judge of fly balls. He had power at the plate, too, but he just couldn't see to hit the ball very often.

There were quite a few good arms around at the time, as a matter of fact: the Phillies' Chuck Klein and Ethan Allen, Pittsburgh's Paul Waner, the White Sox's Mike Kreevich, the Yankees' Ben Chapman. I recall watching relatively obscure outfielders, like the Yankees' Myril Hoag and the Giants' Joe Moore, throw "strikes" to the catcher from medium-deep left center with a man standing in the batter's box. Even Smead Jolley could throw well— once he managed to get his hands on the ball.

My impression is—and there is no way that I can verify it—that baserunning used to be a lot more heedless than it is now. That would mean that there were a lot more targets for fielders to draw a bead on. Runners today are clearly faster, and probably better coached. Whatever the reason, outfielders don't seem to throw as much as they did even thirty years ago.

Plenty of lethal arms have come along in that time and maybe that's the reason the boys are more prudent on the base paths. Among them were Mays, of course, the Phillies' Johnny Callison and Richie Ashburn, Detroit's Al Kaline, the White Sox's Dave Philley, Cleveland's Rocky Colavito, Pittsburgh's Roberto Clemente and Dave Parker, Boston's Carl Yastrzemski, Dwight Evans, and, earlier, Jackie Jensen, Houston's Rusty Staub, and California's Fred Lynn. I must have left out some, I know.

To belabor the obvious, arm strength alone won't do the job. Every high-school coach will tell you that. Quick release and accuracy are equally important. Joe DiMaggio and

Willie Mays had very strong, but sometimes undisciplined, arms. Mel Ott and Roberto Clemente, on the other hand, may have conceded a few yards of distance to others, but threw on a beam of light. Mel's twelve double plays from the outfield in 1929 is still a National League record.

There is an old saying among baseball players and fans that a high total of assists from the outfield may actually be an indication of a weak arm because everyone is running on the fielder. In recent years I have heard this charge made against Mickey Rivers, for example. Old records are of no help at all in sorting out such charges. We are dependent upon the objectivity and long memories of those who were there. All I can add to the subject is the testimony that outfielders I have seen over the years who clearly have strong throwing arms almost invariably have high totals of assists.

The most extraordinary instance on record of an out-fielder throwing with results is Chuck Klein's forty-four assists for the Phillies in 1930. That's about as many as some catchers have for a season. Klein had a good but not spectacular arm, and no one has been able to offer a definitive explanation for the phenomenon of 1930.

Philadelphia fan Joe McGillen, who may have researched the Klein feat more thoroughly than anyone alive, is convinced that the short right-field wall at the old Baker Bowl was a factor, augmented by some mindless baserunning. Almost more significant, McGillen believes, is the classic ineptitude of the Philadelphia pitching staff of that year. They gave up 1,099 runs and 543 walks in 154 games and posted a 6.17 staff ERA. The team also made 239 errors. All Klein had to do was to keep throwing and he was bound to nail someone. It adds some luster to Chuck's achievement—if any is needed—that his teammate Lefty O'Doul was only able to throw out three of that horde from his left-field position.

Obviously, a strong arm is a prime asset in an outfielder, but most directors of player development will concede that a questionable arm will not rule out a candidate if he can compensate for the deficiency with strength in another area—at the plate, for instance. A .350 batting average, 100 RBIs, or 60 stolen bases will usually cause a GM to forget all about arms. Neither Ty Cobb nor Stan Musial had a strong throwing arm, but the fact never jarred the mental calm of their managers, as Ty and Stan were busy driving in close to 4,000 runs between them.

The first axiom of baseball managing must be that adjustments can always be made for a man who swings a destructive bat. Back in the 1920s, the Browns' Baby Doll Jacobson, a lifetime .311 hitter but not strong of arm, used to toss the ball to colleagues Kenny Williams and Jack Tobin to relay to the infield. It's a system that has probably been followed in several dozen outfields since.

One spring back in the 1920s, the ebullient Goose Goslin, then playing for Washington, wrecked his throwing arm by putting the shot to relieve his boredom between turns in the batting cage. By the time the season opened, Goose couldn't have thrown his coat over the back of a chair. Desperate to keep Goslin's big bat in the lineup, manager Bucky Harris assigned a succession of young shortstops to race out into left field to take Goose's beanbag tosses and relay them to the infield. The system may have doomed a few rookie shortstops to early retirement from pernicious exhaustion, but it kept the Goose in the batter's box, where he clocked a league-leading .379 and drove in 102 runs.

Because of the untrammeled character of play in the outfield—the open spaces, the freedom of movement—I would not be surprised if the average fan did not harbor an ideal of the outfielder as the tall, slender athlete, compactly built but fleet of foot and graceful in movement: Fred Lynn, Paul Blair, Jim Landis, Joe DiMaggio, Dode Paskert, Jimmy McAleer. But since outfielders are hired to hit, not to be poetry in motion, what life deals us is Frank Howard at six feet seven and 255 pounds, or Albie Pearson at five feet five and 140 pounds, human storks like Dave Winfield and Dave Kingman, anthropomorphic fire hydrants like Hack Wilson and Dom Dallessandro, and Falstaffs in white flannel like Bob Fothergill. And let's not forget sometime outfielder Yogi Berra, whose figure defies classification. Eddie Gaedel, Bill Veeck's midget, didn't get to stay in the game long enough to draw a fielding assignment on that wonderful afternoon in 1951, but you wouldn't go far wrong betting on left field.

Another reflection of the rich diversity in the outer defense is the nicknames. Country, Suitcase, Foxy Grandpa, Pooch, Ping, Moonlight, Ducky, Motormouth, Frenchy, Tilly, Baby Doll, Turkeyfoot, Glassarm Eddie, Downtown, Bash, Orator, Dim Dom, Scoops, No Neck. Shortstops never attract nicknames like that.

In one of the happiest pieces of clairvoyance on record, the Jones family of Shinglehouse, Pennsylvania, in the summer of 1874, obviated all need for a nickname for their baby boy when they wrote Fielder on the birth certificate. A scant twenty-one summers later, young Fielder Jones was plucking bids for extra bases off the right-field wall at Brooklyn's Eastern Park. Just so Brooklyn fans would not be deceived by his name into thinking that he was a one-dimensional player, Fielder batted .353.

Jones was lucky enough that rookie season to share the grass of Eastern Park with future Hall of Famer Tommy McCarthy, the Leonardo of the trap play, and Mike Griffin, perennial National League fielding-average leader, in what must have been the best outfield ever assembled in the nineteenth century. Early in his career, Jones began to make a thorough study of opposing hitters, and he may have been the first consistent practitioner of positioning in the outfield. It stood him in good stead when he went on to become a playing manager in the newly formed American League and the outstanding center fielder of his generation.

We may exult with the Jones family, but think of the ambitious parents who have bitten the bullet on Theodore Samuel or Tyrus Raymond only to have their scion bat .215 in Little League.

While I am on the subject of diversity in body type and personality in the outfield, I am reminded of how easy it is in discussion to treat all outfielders as though they exercised exactly the same function regardless of position. It's the fallacy of the all-time teams, where the point is for the writer to get the greatest amount of home-run power into a lineup that he knows will never take the field. It should be obvious to even the most casual fan that the center fielder must have the greatest range potential and surest hands since he handles the most chances—anywhere from 10 to 25 percent more than his outfield mates, depending on how assertive he is in running them off balls he can get to. The center fielder should have a good arm, but can sometimes get by if the guys on either side can throw. By contrast, a strong and accurate arm is just about indispensable in a right fielder. And some managers, like the late Casey Stengel, believe that he should be a left-handed thrower. The left fielder can be a big, plodding guy with no arm, some say, if the center fielder can run like the wind and throw like Shoeless Joe Jackson. And so it goes. You may run into as many theories as there are managers. It's not without significance, I think, that the only one-armed ballplayer to make it to the majors, the Browns' Pete Gray, was an outfielder.

Anyone contemplating even the most cursory review of the history of outfielding immediately runs up against the problem of numbers. Outfielders make up one third of every team that takes the field. It would not surprise me to find that since players like Paul Hines, Lipman Pike, and Andy Leonard tussled with line drives bare-handed back in the 1870s, more than a thousand major-league regulars with extended service have been outfielders, among them a lot of outstanding ones. It's a subject for a book in itself.

If I ask myself to name off without reflection the twenty best outfield gloves I have seen, I come up with Joe DiMaggio, Ott, Flood, Mays, Terry Moore, Piersall, Kaline, Blair, Simmons, Cramer, Clemente, Cuyler, Pinson, Vince DiMaggio, Dom DiMaggio, Furillo, Slaughter, Kreevich, Callison, Ashburn. A look into *The Baseball Encyclopedia* reminds me in minutes that I have overlooked players like Lloyd Waner, Sammy West, Ken Berry, Amos Otis, Carl Yastrzemski, Dwight Evans, Sam Chapman, Mickey Stanley, Jim Landis, Fred Lynn, Chet Lemon, any of whom I might want to substitute for those I named if I had more time to think about it. And there may be a dozen more besides.

Look at just those who have played center field in the past hundred years, where, granted, we may expect to find many of the greatest outfielders. In the nineteenth century, besides Fogarty, Welch, Griffin, and Lange, we have Cleveland's Jimmy McAleer, Baltimore's Joe Kelley (in the Hall of Fame) and Steve Brodie, Philadelphia's Hall of Famer "Sliding Billy" Hamilton, and Boston's all-time batting champ, Hugh Duffy. In this century, with two leagues operating full-time for eighty-four years, the names of the great center fielders become a flood. Fielder Jones, of course, and Cleveland's Elmer Flick, the Red Sox's Chick Stahl, Ty Cobb, Rube Oldring, Washington's Clyde Milan, and perhaps the greatest of all, the Red Sox's Tris Speaker, Cincinnati's Dode Paskert, Pittsburgh's Max Carey, the Cubs' Tommy Leach, Edd Roush, Sam Rice, the White Sox's Happy Felsch and later Johnny Mostil, Earle Combs, Lloyd Waner, the Cardinal's Taylor Douthit, the Athletics' Al Simmons, equally great in left, Washington's Sammy West, the Red Sox's Doc Cramer, the Cubs' Kiki Cuyler, Terry Moore, the three DiMaggios, the Athletics' Sam Chapman, Pete Reiser, the Browns' Walt Judnich, the White Sox's Jim Landis and later Ken Berry, the Cubs' Andy Pafko, Brooklyn's Duke Snider, Willie Mays, Mickey Mantle, the Red Sox's Jim Piersall, the Cardinals' Curt Flood, Detroit's Mickey Stanley, Baltimore's Paul Blair, Otis, Lynn, Cedeno, Maddox, Geronimo, and so on. I hope that I have made my point without having to catalog the great ones who played the other two fields.

To acknowledge a bare fraction of the left fielders and right fielders with outstanding gloves, let me point to just those who swung potent enough bats to get themselves into the Hall of Fame, beginning with Babe Ruth, who probably could have played left-handed shortstop if pressed to; Pittsburgh's canny Fred Clarke, who might have made Cooperstown as a manager if he had not been a .315 lifetime hitter; Tommy McCarthy, who teamed with center fielder Hugh Duffy in the combination known to Boston fans of the 1890s as "the Heavenly Twins"; Willie Keeler, diminutive bat-control specialist with the Orioles of the 1890s; Detroit's Sam Crawford, who played alongside Ty Cobb for a dozen years but didn't speak to him except to call for the ball; the Giants' classic right fielder Ross Youngs, succeeded in that spot and followed to the Hall of

Fame by Mel Ott; Brooklyn's Zack Wheat, perhaps the greatest career left fielder in history; more recently, Stan Musial, Al Kaline, Hank Aaron, and Roberto Clemente.

A baseball-writer and fan activity that I don't hear of anymore is selecting all-time outfields who actually played together. I guess there haven't been very many. Right up to World War II, the Red Sox's outfield of 1912 or thereabouts—Harry Hooper, Tris Speaker, and Duffy Lewis— was still being touted as the greatest collection of gloves ever assembled. I don't doubt that they were very good, but naming a "greatest" outfield is tricky. I find it hard to believe that the older trio could have been any better than their Boston successors of 1977—Yastrzemski, Lynn, and Evans—who made just three errors among them and were a scourge to American League base runners. Boston, in fact, must specialize in putting together great outfields. I notice that back in the late 1890s they had Chick Stahl, Hugh Duffy, and Billy Hamilton, all premier center fielders, together for a few seasons.

I would be very hard pressed to name the slickest fielding outfield I have seen in the flesh. Yaz, Lynn, and Evans, perhaps. Musial, Moore, and Slaughter for the Cardinals back in the 1940s were pretty formidable. I also liked Keller, DiMaggio, and Henrich from the same era. It's very hard to judge something like this. For example, I can hardly imagine an outfield better than Pafko, Snider, and Furillo at Brooklyn in the 1950s. But there may have been a combination playing at the same time that could outglove them. Bauer, DiMaggio, and Woodling? It's a tough call.

Undoubtedly, the introduction of gloves produced a revolution of sorts in outfield play. But unfortunately there is little in the records to tell us about it. Initially, gloves must have seemed a more pressing need for infielders and catchers. In studio-posed "action" photos of the late 1880s, outfielders are still shown pursuing fly balls with bare hands. I think it's a safe guess that by the 1890s most outfielders had adopted the use of gloves, although early on some fielders would cut the palms from them.

Progress in outfield play may have been slow in the early days—the numbers suggest that—but as with all other positions, it was inexorable. In 1942, sixty-six years after the founding of the National League, Phillies left fielder Danny Litwhiler played an entire season without making an error—151 games without dropping a fly ball or throwing into the first-base dugout. It was like the four-minute mile. Once Litwhiler had done it, it seemed that almost anyone could. Well, not quite. Only five so far have been able to go for 150 games or more without blemish, among them Rocky Colavito, who survived the full 162 games in 1965. Although he had a great arm, Rocky was never a gazelle in right field. But in 1965, when he handled 274 chances, he managed somehow to stay out of trouble from wire to wire. Not to detract from Colavito's performance in any way, I am most impressed with Curt Flood's 568 chances accepted without error between 1965 and 1967, and California's Brian Downing—a converted catcher—playing 244 consecutive errorless games over three seasons.

If the arrival of gloves didn't produce a significant revolution in outfield play, the appearance of the souped-up ball in 1920 did. "It forced the outfielders back about forty feet," Edd Roush says. "I was used to playing center field somewhere back of second base." Tris Speaker, who may have played the shallowest center field in history, had to yield some, too, but he still stationed himself as near to the infield as any fielder dared. Speaker always maintained that for the handful of balls that were hit over his head in a season he would pick off a hundred line drives that might otherwise have fallen for hits. The record doesn't show it, but I am sure that when Ruth, Meusel, Kenny Williams, Harry Heilmann, and other power hitters began to unload on that rabbit ball in the early 1920s, even "Spoke" must have backed up several feet. The old-fashioned custom of playing shallow may explain why the cutoff wasn't developed until 1922.

Whenever I watch a pop fly bounce about eight feet in the air off an artificial surface, I can't help wondering about the overall effect of Astroturf on outfield play. Paul Mac Farlane, something of a traditionalist in this and other matters, I suspect, has said openly that rugs have ruined the outfield game. To try to get some additional perspective on the matter, I talked with Larry Rojas, outfield instructor at the Phillies' instructional facility in Clearwater, Florida. "It's really not different from playing on grass," Rojas assured me. "In fact, it's easier for an outfielder to charge the ball, since it takes a truer hop." Rojas acknowledges that an outfielder ought to be wary of a high pop that might drop in front of him. He must decide whether to try to smother the hop or to lay back and wait for it to come down. Rojas doesn't see it as a problem for a competent outfielder.

I was most interested in the adjustments that a fielder must make when switching back and forth between Astroturf and grass. "Inconsequential," Rojas says, "especially for a major leaguer. The grass in the big leagues is outstanding." I guess I'll stop worrying about a decline in the quality of play.

There is one thing I can't stop worrying about, though. It is the hair-raising practice of catching all fly balls with one hand, now almost a universal custom. My strongly negative reaction is a sign of age, no doubt. I can't help it. Every time I see one of these young hot dogs camp under a fly with his throwing arm dangling useless at his side, I fight the impulse to close my eyes and pray. In all honesty I can say that I have scarcely ever seen a one-handed specialist drop one. It's all what you get used to, I guess.

Terry Moore, who has a large hand and used an unusually small glove in his playing days, says, "I couldn't catch the ball with one of these jai alai cestas they use today. To me, I always liked to feel the ball. I'd probably have to learn to catch the ball all over again."

There is a story that illustrates the gap in generations on this question. Back in the late 1960s, Rico Carty called forth the disapproval of Atlanta general manager Paul Richards because the big Dominican insisted upon making every catch with one hand. The GM recommended that Rico start catching routine fly balls with two hands. Rico protested that he would be more than happy to except that he didn't know how. Richards made it a direct order. Meekly, Rico retired to left field and when the first high fly headed in his direction, he dutifully raised both hands—and muffed the ball. Ever a man of reason, the Sage of Waxahachie rescinded the order.

For years I have heard it charged that it was Amos Otis who first corrupted the youth of the nation by making the nonchalant, back-of-the-ear catch on fly balls. If I ever did believe that, I don't now. The one-hand catch is generationally endemic, like listening to heavy metal or holding a forefinger outside the glove. I prophesy that sometime in the twenty-first century a young outfielder in a moment of absentmindedness will raise two hands to make a catch— and the media will charge him with hot-dogging.

EDWARD TROWBRIDGE COLLINS. Eddie Collins was the prototype bright, college-educated infielder, who devised defensive strategies based on percentage rather than on cunning. By avoiding the dissipated living common among players of his generation and keeping in top physical condition, Collins extended his playing career through twenty-five major-league seasons. *(National Baseball Library, Cooperstown, N.Y.)*

CHARLES DILLON "CASEY" STENGEL. A good though not great outfielder, Casey wrote the book on playing the tricky right-field wall at Brooklyn's Ebbets Field to the advantage of later Flatbush heroes like Dixie Walker and Carl Furillo. Here he follows the old custom of cutting the palm from his glove to improve the feel of the ball. *(Brown Brothers)*

FLOYD CAVES "BABE" HERMAN. Although it's not entirely certain, some baseball historians believe that this is a shot of Herman loosening up prior to taking his position in the outfield. It is rumored that archivists have yet to unearth a photo of Babe wearing a glove. *(National Baseball Library, Cooperstown, N.Y.)*

WILLIAM HAROLD TERRY. This photo reveals a hint of Bill's graceful movement around the bag. He looks ready to move in any direction to cut off an errant throw, of which, no doubt, he saw many in his era. *(Associated Press photo)*

GEORGE HERMAN "BABE" RUTH. Baseball's greatest pair of eyes zero in on a long drive to right-center field (probably a fungo, in fact). Ruth, as well as successors like Joe DiMaggio, Mel Ott, Willie Mays, Hank Aaron, and others, demonstrated that great sluggers can also be great ball hawks. Babe also had a terrific arm. *(The New York Times)*

JOSEPH PAUL DIMAGGIO. It looks as though the Yankee Clipper is making ready to cut down an imprudent base runner at third or home. You can detect in this shot a bit of that combination of aggressiveness and graceful movement that characterized Joe's play afield. *(Acme Photos/ UPI/Bettmann Archive)*

GORDON STANLEY "MICKEY" COCHRANE. Cochrane was a zealous practitioner of the headlong style of play, kept fresh in recent years by Pete Rose. In this play, Black Mike seems unconcerned that the throw was obviously off-line, and goes after his man with abandon. It looks, however, as though the runner has the throw beaten. *(National Baseball Library, Cooperstown, N.Y.)*

STANLEY CAMFIELD HACK. Classy is the only word to describe the third-base play of Stan Hack in the 1930s and 1940s. Still, he never transcended the gargantuan reputation of the more flamboyant but erratic Pie Traynor—nor has anyone else. Such is the power of legend. *(Acme Photos/ UPI/Bettman Archive)*

WILLIE HOWARD MAYS. Back to the plate at the elongated Polo Grounds, Willie is about to make the most famous catch in World Series history. In game one of the 1954 Series between New York and Cleveland, Mays hauled in Vic Wertz's 475-foot drive to thwart a Cleveland rally. His throw after the catch to hold two Indian base runners was even more remarkable. *(New York* Daily News *photo)*

LOU BOUDREAU. Playing before the era of computers and performance charts, Lou had to analyze batters from his shortstop position the old-fashioned way—he used his head. Worked beautifully, too. And he never experienced a minute of down time. *(Courtesy of the Cleveland Indians)*

LUIS ERNESTO APARICIO. The intrepid Little Looie looks characteristically unconcerned about the threat from hard-charging Horace Clarke, who is already out. What's important is getting that man at first for another double play, one of the more than 1,500 that Aparicio made in his career. *(UPI/ Bettmann Archive)*

BROOKS ROBINSON. In this 1971 World Series photo, Robby has just made another of his legendary diving stops. For the curious, yes, he did scramble to his feet and throw out the runner. *(UPI/Bettmann Archive)*

JESUS MANUEL "MANNY" TRILLO. Manny demonstrates the Flying Wallendas style of infield play that has been causing melancholia among hitters since the 1950s. The photo also points up the deceptive character of modern optics. Actually, the ball eluded Trillo for a run-scoring single. Note that although Manny's glove is not inordinately large, it is all pocket. *(Courtesy of* The Sporting News/*Pat Benic)*

NINE
All Wood and No Leather

"I don't like them fellas who drive in two runs and let in three."

—Casey Stengel

DNA WORKS IN MYSTERIOUS WAYS. A COMPLEX and enigmatic compound, it determines the shape and nature of all living things: the sleek Arabian stallion, the knobby crocodile, the fragile orchid, and the venomous arachnid. But in no instance is DNA's design so startling as in the creation of a baseball player who performs the near impossible feat of batting .350 against major-league pitching but who cannot consistently gather in fly balls or pick up grounders.

There is evidence that the brawny slugger with granite

187

hands has been around since men first began batting and throwing baseballs. For all we know, founder Alex Cartwright himself couldn't be trusted under a pop fly. In the last baseball game played on this earth, a power-hitting third baseman will throw wild to first. Bet on it.

Before the turn of the century, managers and fans did not expect much from the men in the field regardless of how well or poorly they hit. Rarely were managers and fans misled. Sometimes, though, a player would show an imbalance in skills heroic in its proportions—Pete Browning, for example.

When Pete played the outfield for Louisville and several other clubs back in the 1880s and 1890s, he was never heard to talk about anything but hitting. The word was that he slept with his bat. His lifetime batting average of .343 is good enough to place him tenth on the all-time list. In the field it was another story. It was said that Browning could have been replaced in center field by a cigar store Indian to Louisville's advantage. There was always a chance that a drive might bounce off the statue and back to the infield to hold the batter to a double.

When Pete arrived in the majors he was tried at every position except catcher to determine where he would do the least harm. Despairing, Louisville manager Jim Hart finally sent his happy-go-lucky slugger to the outfield. The decision was moot. In 1886, for example, when Browning was well established as one of the American Association's top power hitters, he fielded .791. So far as I can determine, it is the lowest fielding average ever compiled by a major-league player for a full season at any position.

With the exception of Shoeless Joe Jackson, barred from baseball and therefore not eligible, Browning is the only one among the first seventeen players on the all-time batting list who has not been elected to the Hall of Fame.

Maybe I owe the electors an apology. Maybe they are not so enamored of offensive stats as I had supposed.

The gentle Henry Chadwick called butter-fingered oafs like Pete Browning muffins. You can be sure that generations of losing pitchers and ulcer-ridden managers have been calling them something stronger. Whatever you call them, it is worthwhile to note that they come in several forms. First, there are those who could field well if they wanted to but who find interludes with the glove a great bore and a drain on their energies, which are more profitably devoted to hitting. Then there are those who would field if they could but who discover early on that nature has ruled otherwise. They are deserving of compassion. And there are those who couldn't field if they wanted to but who are unconcerned as long as they are hitting twenty homers a season.

Take the case of Ted Williams. You would expect an athlete of his extraordinary eyesight and muscular coordination to become one of the greatest ball hawks of all time. In fact, "Thumper" never could generate enthusiasm for pursuing fly balls. He made little effort to conceal his boredom at having to stand in left field and watch other men bat. Periodically, under prodding from the front office, Williams would make an effort to improve his glove work. But invariably he lost interest as he got caught up in the excitement of yet another race for the batting title.

On one of the rare occasions that Williams was moved to emulate Jim Piersall—in the 1950 All-Star Game—he crashed into the left-field fence at Chicago's Comiskey Park while running down a drive by Ralph Kiner, and broke an elbow. Never short on courage, Ted stayed in the game until the ninth inning, in spite of the pain. Alas, his special effort went for naught, since Kiner later homered to tie the score and the National League went on to win in fourteen innings. Maybe the episode convinced Ted of the vanity of heroics in the field.

It's ironic that it should have been Kiner whom Williams robbed of an extra-base hit—and a bit unfair. Unfair because Ralph never robbed anyone else of a base hit, least of all a fellow slugger. I don't doubt that while there was still spring in his legs, Kiner ran after some things— taxis or blondes, perhaps, but never fly balls.

Curiously, Ty Cobb's notorious compulsion to excel seems not to have followed him into the outfield. Like Williams he clearly had the physical tools, but many contemporary accounts show him to have been a mercurial fielder at best. When the mood was on him he would make spectacular plays. At other times he appeared bored with having to wait for another turn at bat, and occasionally he amused himself (and worried the Detroit fans) by catching fly balls atop his cap without looking the ball into the glove. It takes more than the length of Cobb's career to explain a twentieth-century record of 271 errors by an obviously competent outfielder.

The problem for the muffin who can but won't field is that he cannot mitigate his sins with the glove by being good copy. Never will he generate the kind of nostalgic affection that we heap on colorful fumblers like Babe Herman, Zeke Bonura, and Marv Throneberry. I can't imagine a reporter telling the story of, say, Willie McCovey or "Moose" Skowron, as Jimmy Breslin did of Marv Throneberry that the team wanted to give him a cake for his birthday but decided against it because they were afraid that he would drop it. The extraordinary thing about the Throneberry legend is that it was the creation of a single glorious season. Marv's former managers and teammates attest that he was a dependable journeyman with the glove before he arrived at the Polo Grounds in 1962 to bid for immortality with Casey Stengel's Mets.

No player in history has contributed more tales to the canon of creative fielding than Babe Herman. And it's just possible that every one of them is true. As former Dodger scout Fresco Thompson pointed out, Herman wore a glove for only one reason: It was the league custom.

One of my favorite stories about Herman goes back to 1930, one of the rare occasions when a Brooklyn team of that era was in contention for the pennant late in the season. In the ninth inning of an important game in Cincinnati, Babe misplayed a soft liner into a base-clearing triple and the Dodgers lost by one run. In the locker room after the game, the big outfielder sat with his head buried in his hands, apparently inconsolable over his misdemeanor in the field. Coming upon the dejected figure, losing-pitcher Hollis Thurston quickly put aside his anger and resentment. His heart went out to his grieving teammate and he put a consoling hand on Herman's shoulder. Before Thurston could tell Herman to put the incident behind him, Babe looked up and wailed, "Jeez, if that last drive I hit had fallen in, I'd be hitting .370."

For all their peccadilloes afield, some muffins are so winning in personality, so waiflike in their helplessness under fly balls, that only the most icy-hearted manager or pitcher would decline to forgive and forget, especially when the offender is more than likely to weigh in with a couple of tape-measure home runs in the next game. Reggie Jackson is like that. So was Greg Luzinski before he escaped to the American League and the sanctuary of the designated-hitter (DH) rule. They say that "the Bull" is still missed in left field at Philadelphia's Veterans Stadium—particularly by the gap hitters on visiting clubs.

Sure I remember that Reggie almost suffered a skull fracture from a fly ball in game four of the 1981 World Series and opened the flood gates for Los Angeles. But he's of such even temperament that he would never let a little thing like that affect his hitting. He had a perfect night at the plate.

Rivaling Babe Herman in the affections of many old-timers is Smead Jolley, the oversized, easygoing Arkansan, who played the outfield for the White Sox and later the Red Sox in the early 1930s. Considering the brevity of his major-league career—four seasons—Smead left a remarkable legacy with his glove. In the minors he was so inept in the field that even after he had registered successive batting marks of .397, .404, and .387 with San Francisco in the Pacific Coast League and had driven in 510 runs, no major-league club would touch him. Finally, in 1930, the White Sox, a chronic loser in that era, made an institutional sign of the cross and purchased Jolley's contract.

In his first season at Chicago, Smead hit .313, batted in 114 runs, and made history with his glove. After a particularly bad half-inning in right field he would waddle into the dugout mumbling, "Bad sky today. Not a single angel up there to help out old Smudge." The most widely circulated story of his misadventures in the field, repeated by witnesses as sober as Bill Dickey and illustrator Gene Mack, had Jolley making three errors on one play. First, he let a single go between his legs and roll to the fence. As he turned to retrieve the ball, it bounced off the fence and went through his legs a second time. Smead finally ran down the elusive ball only to throw wild to third, permitting everyone to score.

Great story. The trouble is that it's not true. I don't doubt that the play unfolded exactly as described. A lot of people saw it. But evidently the official scorer that day was not so brutal as to charge the unhappy Smead with three errors. Nowhere in the records will you find him down for three in one inning, not to speak of three on one play. Only Hall of Famer Harry Heilmann managed three in one inning.

Apparently, Jolley couldn't avoid mishaps even when he was throwing, which was his strong suit defensively. When he was traded to the Red Sox in 1932, the Boston coaching staff drilled him carefully on how to play Fenway Park's notorious incline in left field, known as Duffy's Hill (now gone). Big Smudge conscientiously practiced shagging flies while running up the slope toward the wall until he could have done it in his sleep. In his first test under game conditions he raced up the incline as he had been taught and smartly plucked a potential extra-base hit off the wall. So elated was he at making the catch that as he stepped toward the infield to make a throw, he forgot the slope and fell flat on his face. No one seems to recall whether any runners advanced.

Perhaps the most lovable of all fumbling outfielders in the old days was Frank "Lefty" O'Doul, a sunny-dispositioned Irishman from San Francisco, who saw service with all three New York teams and a couple of other clubs as well. Errors never ruffled the calm of Lefty's existence. Neither did curve balls. Had he not fallen just short of the required 4,000 at-bats, O'Doul's .349 lifetime average would have placed him fourth on the all-time batting list. In 1929, he missed .400 by just two percentage points. His 254 hits that season set a National League record which still stands. Whenever Lefty picked up a bat he struck terror into the hearts of pitchers. Whenever he slipped on a glove, pitchers trembled too—his own.

There is a story that when O'Doul was with the Giants a New York City bar owner called the Polo Grounds to complain that Lefty's check had bounced. Since the outfielder ran his social life strictly on a cash basis, he knew that he had not written the check. He was equally certain that he had never set foot in the bar in question, drunk or sober. Nevertheless, he agreed to hurry downtown and check into the matter.

The minute Lefty walked through the swinging doors and introduced himself, the barkeeper realized that he had taken the bad check from an impostor. He apologized to the ballplayer. The good-natured O'Doul offered to make good the check anyway and stood a couple of rounds for the lads sitting at the bar. Then he admonished the bartender. "If some fellow comes in here again in the dim light, says he's Lefty O'Doul and wants to cash a check, you just take him across the street to the empty lot and hit him a couple of fungoes. If he catches them, don't take his check. It's definitely not O'Doul."

It's fascinating the way the whims of general managers can sometimes produce improbable lineups. When O'Doul moved from Philadelphia to Brooklyn in 1931, he found himself in the same outfield with, yes, Babe Herman. In center field, sandwiched between such titans of ineptitude, the normally steady journeyman Johnny Frederick came all unglued and wound up leading the league in errors himself. But the idea that Brooklyn actually came within one year of being able to field Herman, O'Doul, and Hack Wilson together is more than the imagination can bear.

Maybe it's unfair to mention Hack Wilson in the same breath with O'Doul and Herman. Opinions on Hack's fielding are mixed. There are stories enough, to be sure, about Hack's mishaps in the field, notably the disaster that overtook him and the Cubs in game four of the 1929 World Series, when he lost three fly balls in the course of the game (he was charged with only one error) and the Athletics overcame an 8–0 Chicago lead. On the other hand, Wilson's former managers, some of the most hard-nosed in the history of the game—McGraw, McCarthy, Hornsby, Carey, Stengel—usually spoke well of his play. Of course, it's not hard to become fond of a guy who can drive in 190 runs in one season and bat .356 while he's doing it. My guess is that what McGraw and the other disciplinarians liked about Hack was that however unpredictable his glove, he never failed to hustle after a ball hit in his direction.

I only saw Wilson once or twice, toward the end of his career. I have shadowy recollections of a gray-clad nail keg scurrying about on barely discernible legs. Any problems Hack had in the field could have been attributed in part to his strange physique. The former boilermaker stood a scant five feet six and weighed upward of 190 pounds, none of it fat. From the belt up he had the size and strength of an NFL linebacker. In his lower half he was Tinkerbell. It was commonly reported that Wilson supported that massive torso on the smallest feet in organized baseball. I read somewhere that Mel Ott's first major-league home run was a low liner that Hack tried to shoestring only to have it skip through his legs for four bases. That's hard to believe. There wasn't room enough for a ball to skip between Hack's legs.

Perhaps Wilson's best known contribution to baseball folklore involves a game that the Dodgers played at Philadelphia's storied Baker Bowl. As best I can figure, the year must have been 1933. Brooklyn manager, Casey Stengel, had gone to the mound to remove a large and highly temperamental pitcher named "Boom-Boom" Beck, who was being rudely handled by the Phillies' power-laden batting order. In right field, Wilson, reputed to be one of baseball's connoisseurs of sour mash, was nursing a heroic hangover. Beck protested long and loud about being lifted, and refused to surrender the ball to his manager.

Hack took advantage of the stormy interlude to bend over with his hands on his knees and close his eyes in hopes that shutting out the sun might ease the throbbing in his temples.

At the mound, Stengel was demanding the ball and threatening to suspend his irascible pitcher if he did not get it. Instead of handing Casey the ball, Beck hurled it against the right-field wall (at Baker Bowl a seven-iron shot from the infield). Hearing the thud behind him, Hack snapped to life, turned, fielded the carom, and threw a strike to third to keep the phantom runner from advancing. Stengel swore that it was the best throw Hack had made all season.

Since Herman, O'Doul, and Wilson never did come together, my choice for history's all-time, all-wood outfield is Detroit's 1920s trio of Harry Heilmann, Heinie Manush, and Fat Bob Fothergill. In a combined total of forty-two major-league seasons, the three averaged .333 and drove in more than 3,300 runs. In 1926, their collective average was .371, and Tiger manager Ty Cobb felt obliged to bench himself to keep from weakening the team's offense. Cobb hit a sickly .340 for the portion of the season that he played.

If Heilmann, Manush, and Fothergill punished American League pitching, they punished their bathroom scales even more. The outfield dressed out at somewhere around 650 pounds. One day when Fothergill was batting at Yankee Stadium, Leo Durocher, then a brash rookie in Yankee pinstripes, asked the umpire to call time and complained that it was illegal to have two men in the batter's box. The choleric Fothergill promptly struck out.

It was not that the ponderous Tigers bobbled so many balls, though they held up their end in what was a more tolerant age. It was that their size did not permit them to get to everything. I wonder if anyone has ever checked on how many triples Detroit gave up in the 1920s.

To illustrate why general managers have a slightly shorter life expectancy than sky divers, in 1928 Detroit traded Manush to St. Louis for Harry Rice, who was a petite 185 pounds and could run. Naturally, Rice could hit, too. In those days the Tigers probably wouldn't have issued a uniform to an outfielder who was batting under .340. The bad news was that Rice proved to be a worse fielder than any of the three behemoths who had been patrolling the grass at Navin Field. And Manush revealed his pique at being traded by batting .378 for St. Louis and making only three errors in 154 games.

Not content with this disastrous attempt to bring speed and chic to the Tiger outfield, the Detroit front office benched Fothergill the following season and replaced him with rookie Roy Johnson, very fast afoot and a near wraith at 175 pounds. Young Johnson hit well, of course, but he made a catastrophic thirty-one errors, still an American League record for outfielders. In the course of the season, manager Bucky Harris, then in his first year at Detroit, was observed to gray rapidly around the temples though he was barely thirty. He not only had Johnson and Rice to worry about, but also Dale Alexander at first and Heinie Schuble, who fielded .886 that season, at short. (Yes, the Tigers led the league in hitting with .299). One day after Johnson had dropped a routine fly, he slunk back to the dugout, an apology forming on his lips. "Forget it, kid," Harris said. "The ball hit you in a bad spot—the middle of your glove."

Heavy bats and stiff fingers seemed to run in the Johnson family. Roy's younger brother, Bob, a prodigious slugger with the Athletics and later with the Red Sox, used to cause incipient heart failure among bleacher fans at Shibe Park whenever he maneuvered under a fly ball. But after some years in the league, Bob more or less got the hang of things and finished his career without sustaining a head injury from a falling baseball.

For all the hoary axioms about the advantages of speed in the outfield, it's not the solution to every fly catcher's problems. Take Lou Brock and Ron LeFlore, to name just two super speedsters who had their share of problems with the glove. Brock, arguably the fastest man ever to play the game, could get to the ball without difficulty. The question was what was he to do once he got there. Lou's seven seasons leading the National League's outfielders in errors is a major-league record and looks as unassailable as DiMaggio's consecutive-game hitting streak. Only Reggie Jackson seemed for a time to have an outside chance of overtaking Brock. But he was rescued by the designated-hitter rule.

As a matter of fact, the advent of the DH rule brought a new form of muffin into being—the muffless muffin, or the natural-born designated hitter. Countless slugging heroes from the past—Pete Browning, for example—might have qualified as natural-born DHs had they not suffered the misfortune of being born too soon. Lucky Hal McRae, on the other hand, has been treated more kindly by history, and with the near certainty that he will finish out his distinguished batting career with a lifetime average of more than .290, he presently ranks as our greatest living natural-born DH.

When a manager pencils in the name of Dwight Evans, Dwayne Murphy, or Chet Lemon to DH, he is spreading around an unwelcome but necessary chore, like taking out the garbage or washing the family car. But when he assigns the task to a Hal McRae, a Dave Kingman, or a Greg Luzinski, he taps not a ballplayer, but an athlete uniquely designed by nature to swing a home-run bat for a pitcher and do nothing else. At a stroke of the pencil a manager can strengthen his club both offensively and defensively.

It's curious how often natural-born DHs have made their appearances in the National League, which has not adopted the DH rule, and with God's help never will. Of course, how else would we have learned that they were natural-born and not rote DHs? McRae, for example, fielded .833 in his last year at Cincinnati, thereby marking out his true destiny. The Reds shipped him off to Kansas City and the American League, where he was to bring an early luster to the newly promulgated DH rule. To demonstrate that Hal was truly natural-born and not an impostor, the injury-riddled Royals dusted off a glove a few seasons back and sent their DH out to do battle with fly balls. He fielded .500—two chances, one error.

It's understandable that managers should love the natural-born DH. But, as sometimes happens in life, you can have too much of a good thing. A club may find itself blessed with two or more, and, to date, American League rules allow for only one at a time in the batting order. The White Sox, to cite an instance, suffer a surfeit of riches with Greg Luzinski and Ron Kittle, not to mention Tom Paciorek and perhaps one or two others. In Kansas City, Willie Aikens spent years patiently awaiting the retirement of McRae before being shipped off to Toronto, where he was challenged to outlive Cliff Johnson.

The most striking example of a natural-born DH brought into this world before his time is Russell "Buzz" Arlett, who achieved a major-league career of one season with the Phillies in 1931. There are no funny stories about Arlett, only sad ones. During batting practice before a spring exhibition game a year or two after Philadelphia had sent him back to the minors, despite his .313 batting average and eighteen homers, Buzz awed the New York Yankee bench by hitting a dozen pitches out of sight while using both sides of the plate. "Wow," Yankee outfielder Ben Chapman responded, "how come the Phillies let that big guy go, and why doesn't somebody pick him up quick? Like us maybe?" "Just wait a little bit and you'll see," manager Joe McCarthy said. Sure enough, in the first inning, a Yankee batter lifted a high, lazy fly to right field, where Arlett, staggering under the ball for a few seconds, finally muffed it for a three-base error.

Arlett must be the most bewildering case of imbalance in skills in the history of baseball. In a minor-league career that spanned almost 2,400 games, all but a handful spent in what we would now call Triple-A, the switch-hitting Arlett batted .341, hit 432 home runs, and drove in 1,786 runs. He also stole 200 bases. Like his contemporary, Babe Ruth, Buzz began his career as a pitcher, and from 1919 through 1922 he averaged 24 wins a season for Oakland of the Pacific Coast League and had an ERA of 3.45. What is most puzzling is that Arlett was widely regarded among West Coast baseball writers as a good-fielding pitcher.

In time, Arlett, like Babe Ruth before him, was shifted from the mound to the outfield to keep his bat in the lineup every day. Buzz appeared to be another Ruth in every respect but one. He could not catch a fly ball.

In spite of Arlett's poor fielding, the sound of his bat could not long be disregarded by major-league clubs back East. In 1924, he hit .328 on 229 hits, including 57 doubles, 19 triples, and 33 homers. He also had 145 runs batted in and stole 22 bases. Even in the hit-happy 1920s, no major-league front office could overlook numbers like that. Soon the Cardinals, among other teams, were hot on his trail. There is a story that during the games in which St. Louis scouted him, Arlett loafed egregiously in the field and was actually hit on the head by a fly ball. The Cardinals and others lost interest and Buzz continued to set Pacific Coast League batting records as he languished at Oakland.

By 1929, the big guy had really shifted his bat into high gear. He batted .374 on 270 hits, 70 of them doubles and 39 home runs. He had 189 RBIs and 22 stolen bases. Incredibly, no major-league club was yet ready to sign him. Could anyone have been so dreadful in the field?

In the following year, Brooklyn, a team not known to put too fine a point on defensive skills—they already had O'Doul and Herman—began to scout Arlett seriously. After a hard look, they signed Ike Boone instead. This was the ultimate insult. Ike's glove was pure Teflon. It was comparable to signing Roy Johnson over Smead Jolley.

In 1931, the Phillies, mired for years in the second division and having nothing to lose, bought Arlett's contract. They also owned the coziest park in the majors, which seemed ideally suited to Arlett's switch-hitting power. It may be that at age thirty-two, Buzz was disheartened from the years of neglect, but the Phillies could not have had complaints about his hitting. He batted over .300 and finished fourth in the league in home runs. His fielding marks for 1931 seem innocuous enough. The only clue we have to the reason for Arlett's hasty return to the minors is that an old-time Philadelphia bartender once told Jimmy Breslin that every time Buzz caught up with a fly ball and then held on to it, Phillies fans marched to their favorite speakeasies and got roaring drunk in celebration. Securely back in Triple-A in 1932, Buzz did some celebrating himself—54 homers and 144 RBIs.

Someone may get the impression from this chronicle that managers automatically assign muffins to the outfield and pray that their pitcher will induce all batters to hit ground balls. Not so. There is a time-honored tradition of using first base as a sanctuary, starting with Cap Anson, who was his own manager and knew a thing or two about hiding muffins. On occasion a muffin will surface at third or behind the plate with predictable results. Rare indeed is the manager bold enough to send one to the middle infield, where damage could prove irreparable. But it has happened.

Detroit's Rudy York offers a good case study in the problems of keeping a muffin out of harm's way between turns at bat. The big, easygoing Indian from Georgia, once described by Tom Meany as part Cherokee and part first baseman, arrived in Motown in 1937, the year after manager Mickey Cochrane had suffered a near-fatal beaning at Yankee Stadium, an accident that ended his catching career. Immediately, Cochrane had Rudy measured for mask and pads just to see what would happen. When Mickey could no longer bear to watch, he shifted York to third base. The experience was even more painful. However, Rudy eased some of the boss's pain by hitting 35 homers in just 375 at-bats, which included a record 18 round-trippers in August.

Eager to keep York in the lineup, Cochrane next tried him in the outfield. Of that experience Rudy himself commented that the commissioner's office should have granted him special dispensation to wear a catcher's mask in right field. First base was the obvious refuge. But it was already occupied by future Hall of Famer Hank Greenberg, who had known his own travails learning to play the bag. Always a class guy, Greenberg volunteered to move his big frame to the outfield and begin a new apprenticeship

so that the Tigers could benefit from York's bat. In his
spare time, Hank even instructed Rudy on how to mini-
mize his problems at first base.

Rudy York's pilgrimage is nothing compared to that of
"Piano Legs" Hickman. Rudy, after all, did find a home in
a season or two. In six seasons early in this century,
Hickman changed teams six times and changed positions
twenty-three times as a succession of frantic managers
sought to keep him out of the path of batted balls while
they enjoyed the benefits of his thundering bat. In 1900,
his rookie year, Piano Legs made eighty-six errors at
third base in 120 games and helped to drive manager Buck
Ewing into early and permanent retirement even before
the season was over. Ewing's successor, George Davis,
was so mesmerized by Hickman's long-ball hitting that it
took until September for him to notice that the kid was
not going to cut it at the hot corner. In time, Piano Legs
solved the problem for everyone. He went into an irre-
versible batting slump.

Like George Davis, most managers will suffer any out-
rage from a muffin so long as he keeps making music with
the bat. Not all managers, however. In 1923, a young outfielder named Moe Solomon, a native of New York City,
tore up the Southwestern League with his bat. Playing for
the Hutchinson club, he had forty-nine home runs, more
than anyone else in organized baseball that season, including Babe Ruth. In New York, Giant manager John
McGraw's eyes gleamed as he envisioned a Jewish power
hitter established at the cozy Polo Grounds and the city's
large Jewish population storming the the turnstiles for a
chance to watch Moe swat home runs. Without even scouting the kid, McGraw shelled out the then considerable sum
of $4,500 for Solomon's contract and brought him to New
York toward the end of the season.

At bat Moe was everything that could be expected of a kid out of Class B. He hit National League pitching at a .375 pace. Unfortunately, his fielding average wasn't much higher. What the front office in Hutchinson had neglected to report as they banked McGraw's check was that Moe couldn't snare a Ping-Pong ball with an empty swimming pool. Before the first leaf had fallen in 1923, the kid was on his way back to Class B, never to return to the majors.

You have to wonder how long McGraw would have tolerated someone like the Pirates' Dick Stuart, who in the 1960s won the title of Dr. Strangeglove. It was said of Stuart that he had no health-threatening habits. He did not drink, smoke, stay up late, or get in the path of ground balls. But between bobbles, Dick hit 228 home runs, and that helped him cling to a major-league spot for ten seasons. That's the bottom line in a muffin's contract with society. He must deliver the long ball with some regularity.

In the late 1950s, the White Sox brought up a six-feet-seven, 225-pound rookie named Ron Jackson, whose travel bag contained a largely unscarred first baseman's mitt. During spring training, Ted Williams among others predicted that young Jackson would become one of the most feared batters in baseball. It was true. And the fear engendered when he stepped into the batter's box was in his manager, who had a wife and kids to support. Worse, when Ron took the field, White Sox fans began to chant, "Bring back Bonura." If Jackson had been able to hit like Zeke, as well as field like him, there would have been no chanting. After several futile seasons, Jackson disappeared into the mist, leaving behind a .245 lifetime batting average and a record of just seventeen home runs.

There is something about truly dreadful fielding that

cries out for commemoration. In their fashion, the Pete Brownings, the Smead Jolleys, and the Zeke Bonuras have warmed more hearts than would a carload of journeyman shortstops. I propose that a quiet, elm-shaded site at Cooperstown be set aside in memory of those who have proved to us through the years that cutting down the tying run at home is not the most important thing in life. Let it be a kind of poets' corner of muffindom.

I think, too, there should be a memorial piece in pink granite, two large hands reaching heavenward in the clamshell position. And seeming to trickle down the knuckles of one hand, perhaps, a baseball fashioned of pure alabaster. Below, on a slender pedestal of Bedford limestone, should be inscribed the names of those who have so earnestly reached for the ball in their lifetime and mostly come up with air:

> Willie Mays Aikens
> David Dale Alexander
> Adrian Constantine Anson
> Russell Loris Arlett
> Don Edward Baylor
> Adelphia Louis Bissonette
> Ronald Mark Blomberg
> Henry John Bonura
> Isaac Morgan Boone
> Louis Clark Brock
> Louis Rogers Browning
> Jesse Cail Burkett
> Louis Peo Chiozza
> Michael Joseph Donlin
> John Joseph Doyle
> Francis John Fennelly

George Farley Grantham
James Raymond Hart
Floyd Caves Herman
Charles Taylor Hickman
James Francis Hogan . . .

On second thought, better make that a broad pedestal.

TEN

Solomon in the Press Box

"There's no such thing as a bad hop. It's the way you played it."

—Leo Durocher

TOP OF THE EIGHTH, TWO OUT, MAN ON THIRD. River City trails three to one. With the visitors' hard-hitting but slow-footed third baseman at bat, the count has gone to two and two. On the mound, River City's loose-jointed, six-feet-nine Lefty McHeeter holds the ball in his glove and squints toward the plate for the sign. It doesn't much matter what the catcher calls for. Lefty has already walked nine, hit two batsmen, and made two wild pitches. These details pale before the central fact that Lefty has given up no hits.

Yes, River City's own is within four outs of pitching a "masterpiece." (Before the age of television they were simply called no-hitters. Now that they occur much more frequently, they are invariably masterpieces or classics.) It's quite possible that no one present has ever seen a no-hitter. The last one pitched at River City was in 1930. The fans hold their breath on every pitch. So do the visiting players—out of fear of decapitation. Lefty's 98-mph-plus fastball is everywhere but in the strike zone.

The big pitcher nods, then comes forward in that great sweeping motion. The batter hits a grass cutter just to the right of second, on which River City's second baseman makes a diving backhand stop. Seated on his double knits, the infielder has trouble getting the ball out of the webbing of his glove, drops the ball, recovers, makes a perfect throw to first. Late by a millisecond. The runner scores from third.

In another era many fans might have looked toward the press box to see whether the official scorer would raise an index finger to indicate a hit or make a circle with index and thumb to signal an error. In today's giant ball parks a fan would be lucky even to locate the press box. The River City faithful fix their attention on the electronic scoreboard in center field.

After a nail-biting delay of sixty-seven seconds, the message "Error" pulsates on the big screen. Cheers, sighs. Lefty's classic is intact. Four more outs and he will have pitched a no-hitter in this, his first (and possibly last) season in the majors. The lanky pitcher grins. The second baseman nods approval to the press box. It is, after all, only his fifth error of the season. The batter alone has cause to be unhappy with the call. In fact, he is content with getting in the run and escaping River City with his batting helmet unshattered.

Did River City's official scorer shade his decision in favor of Lefty and the home team, in the interest, perhaps, of ensuring his safe passage from the ball park to his suburban home? No, not necessarily. True, the second baseman's diving catch was more than ordinary effort on a hard chance. But having made the stop, he could easily have thrown out one of the league's most notoriously slow runners had he not fumbled the ball when taking it from his glove. Moreover, it is one of the oldest traditions in scoring that in the late innings the first hit must be a clean one. The call might have gone either way and not been considered inconsistent with the scoring rules.

An official scorer is not likely to be called on more than once in a long career to make a decision as weighty as one affecting a no-hitter. In almost every game he scores, however, he will have to make several judgment calls that can affect a player's day-to-day record of performance, including hits, errors, and earned runs. In this way the scorer does influence the opinion of both the front office and the fan about the ability of individual players. Unlike the umpires, the official scorer makes no decisions that affect the outcome of the game. But he presides with arbitrary power over the compilation of the record of the game, the raw material of the statistics by which all players survive or perish. It would be surprising if such a system did not generate some controversy. The real surprise is that it has generated so little.

One of the most remarkable facts about a remarkable game is that baseball's scoring rules governing what constitutes a hit or an error have remained essentially unchanged for more than a hundred years. The language in today's rule book is somewhat more expansive and it offers a bit more specific counsel to scorers, but the concept is the same. The explanation of the conditions under which

a batter should be given a base hit as it appears in the
National League Playing Rules for 1878 (the oldest I could
lay hands on) is worth repeating in full:

> When the ball from the bat strikes the ground
> between the foul-lines and out of reach of the
> fielders.

> When a hit is partially or wholly stopped by a
> fielder in motion, but such player cannot recover
> himself in time to handle the ball before the
> striker reaches first base.

> When a ball is hit so sharply to an infielder that
> he cannot handle it in time to put out a man. *In
> case of doubt over this class of hits, score a base
> hit and exempt fielder from the charge of an er-
> ror.* [Emphasis added.]

> When a ball is hit so slowly toward a fielder that
> he cannot reach it before the batsman is safe.

Really nothing equivocal here. Look in the 1985 edition
of the official rule book and you will find that it uses more
words to say the same thing. It says to me that if since
the earliest days of professional baseball the scorer has
been enjoined to rule in the batter's favor on plays where
there is doubt, undeserved hits may be common in the
history of the game, but undeserved errors are probably
rare. This is important for anyone trying to make an estimate of the quality of fielding in the past because whatever the limitations of fielding average as a measure of a
player's defensive ability, it is the principal criterion available from the earliest days to the present. I find nothing
in the rules to suggest that because the playing surfaces of

a hundred years ago were of poorer quality than today's, fielders were casually charged with errors on bad hops.

Fred Lieb, whose career as a baseball writer began about 1910, was among those guilty of explaining away the poor fielding records of nineteenth-century players. On a number of occasions he characterized the scorer of the early days as a cold-hearted autocrat who would charge a man with an error "if he so much as got a finger-nail on the ball." Short of reviewing ten miles of nonexistent videotape, how could Lieb have been so sure of this? Chances are he spent a lot of time talking with old ball-players who were still brooding over hits they had been "robbed" of thirty years earlier.

Lieb's sweeping charge against the early scorers makes no sense. To begin with, they would have been acting against the letter of the scoring rules. And to what advantage? There is abundant evidence that the average base-ball player of the nineteenth century was a hard-boiled, often hard-drinking fellow of limited education with a distinct penchant for violence on and off the field. If such a character was quick to menace an umpire over a called strike, how would he react to a scorer who had robbed him of a precious base hit, especially when the rules so patently supported his case? Why should a scorer invite bodily harm when it would be so much easier to follow the rules and at the same time make the batter (and the fielder) happy? As implicit evidence that players were not averse to busting a nose or two over a lost base hit, we know that most clubs went to considerable lengths to keep the identity of the scorer secret. Chicago even went so far as to assign a woman to score for many years, presumably as an additional step toward providing the scorer with deep cover.

When I read that Bill Shindle, shortstop for the Philadelphia entry in the Players League in 1890, made 119 errors in just 132 games, while his rival, Jack Rowe, made only 67 errors for Buffalo, playing on the same fields and with the same equipment, I can only conclude that Bill wasn't a very good shortstop. In truth he was not a shortstop at all, but a converted third baseman who soon returned to his regular position, where he performed not brilliantly, but somewhat better. He was a pretty good double-play man at both positions.

The Players League, incidentally, was no humpty-dumpty outfit. It was formed by a collection of the top stars of the National League and the American Association, who were on strike against organized baseball's reserve clause. Although it survived only one year, it may have been the most talent-rich league ever assembled. If this declaration seems at variance with Shindle's palpable inability to pick up ground balls, let me explain that Bill was one of the league's top power hitters and tied for third in home runs. Shindle hit .322, Rowe .250. It's all a matter of priorities.

I am further persuaded that scorers of the nineteenth century were on the whole a competent and fair-minded lot by the fact that as early as 1889 they formed a professional organization, the Scorers League, to codify practices. That doesn't sound like the action of a gang of fanged villains, intent on saddling the Bill Shindles of the world with a one-hundred-plus errors a season.

On the matter of professionalism, I am impressed, too, by a letter of instruction to official scorers in 1887 from National League president Nicholas E. Young. The year 1887, by the way, was one in which several experimental rules were on the books, including those which allowed the batter a fourth strike and credited him with a hit for a base on balls. "A ball player," Young writes, "has no appeal from the decision of a scorer as to a base hit, an error or an assist, yet these points, insignificant in themselves, go to make up the record upon which the player to a great degree depends for reputation and employment. The temptation to assist players of the local team by granting hits and exempting fielders from errors is frequently alluring, and nothing would be more natural than an occasional yielding thereto, though I believe the official corps to be animated by a genuine spirit of fairness."

Further along in his letter, Young deals with specific game situations and offers broad counsel on how they should be scored. And then he concludes: "I have been asked where the line of demarcation lies between a base hit for a batsman and an error for a fielder. . . . The distinction is frequently so fine as to be a matter of opinion, though a few general considerations should govern a majority of cases. In the first place I would adopt the player's standpoint in scoring hits. It is of course impossible for the scorer to accurately estimate the ability of each particular fielder, nor can he tell whether the players are in good form. While these important points cannot weigh with the reporter, he can judge as to the honesty and sincerity of the effort made, and the results obtained should be considered in that light. "Record players" are soon recognized and should be unsparingly dealt with. The fielder of the future is the man who tries for everything and allows his average to look out for itself."

In tone and substance, Young's letter is a model directive to a group of sports officials having to make tough judgment calls, and aside from a touch of archaism in the language, it could be circulated without offense and with profit to today's official scorers. With the kind of supervision and guidance implied by the directive, I can't help believing that scoring a hundred years ago was pretty sound and professional, and that the records generally reflect the abilities of the players.

I am not suggesting that there haven't been abuses in scoring through the long history of the game, especially ones involving the awarding of cheap hits. There is a well-supported story that the colorful Colonel Bozeman Bulger of *The New York World* once awarded an unidentified hit to Giant second baseman Larry Doyle because it had to be assigned to someone, and as Bulger said, "Larry is a nice guy." At the end of the season that hit helped make Doyle the National League batting champion. An infinitely more egregious example of irresponsible scoring was the awarding of eight cheap bunt hits to Larry Lajoie near the end of the 1910 season during a thinly disguised conspiracy by players and managers to cheat Ty Cobb of the batting title. (Cobb won it anyway.)

I frequently read—and have been reading since I first started following baseball—that standards of scoring have gone to pot. Most often the charges are made by retired baseball writers and have to do with fine points, such as the too generous awarding of sacrifice hits. Obviously, I am not in a position to judge the soundness of the complaints. If I had to make a fan's appraisal of changes in scoring over a long period of years, I would say that scorers are somewhat stricter about awarding hits on borderline plays than they were forty years ago, an ancillary effect, I suspect, of the availability of instant replay. Although I should hasten to add that a baseball official said to me not long ago that everything tends to look like an error on instant replay.

Let me offer an example. In the National League playoff series a couple of seasons back, the Dodgers' Fernando Valenzuela hit a tremendous drive to right center at Dodger Stadium. The Phillies' Garry Maddox got a good jump on the ball, ran about two city blocks to catch up with it, and was just about to glove the ball when he slipped on the muddy warning track and fell down. He drew a three-base error on the play. Maddox was not pleased, of course, but he took it stoically. The TV cameras later showed Valenzuela near apoplexy in the dugout after someone told him that he had been denied a triple.

I asked Watson Spoelstra, who covered the Tigers for the *Detroit News* from 1946–1972, about changes in the quality of scoring since he has been following baseball. "In my judgment," he said, "baseball scoring has remained remarkably sound. About the time I retired there was a transition period brought about by many newspapers barring their experienced writers from scoring duties. I thought there would be a scoring decline, but there wasn't." Both Spoelstra and Allen Lewis, who retired from *The Philadelphia Inquirer* in 1979, believe that there may be more pressure on scorers today because of the proliferation of bonus clauses in player contracts attached to specific achievements. When the difference between 200 hits for the season and 199 may be $100,000, a player is likely to be even more emotional about each one than when only prestige is at stake. But Lewis, too, rejects the idea that there has been any general deterioration in scoring.

I said earlier that it is surprising how little controversy the scoring system has given rise to. I meant relative to the numbers of players involved in professional baseball and the length of time that it has been played. Certainly there has been evidence of grousing by individual players going far back in the history of the game. In a democratic society there is something about an apparently arbitrary decision that is bound to cause discontent, especially when it directly affects someone's livelihood. As long ago as 1912, *Baseball Magazine* felt moved to editorialize:

> There is nothing unimportant in the work of the official scorer. Upon his work, to a greater or lesser degree, rests the reputation of every baseball player and his work can, without stretching a point, change a star into a near star or a discard into a possibility.

It has been suggested more than once that what helps save the system is the length of the season. Over the course of 154 or 162 games small inequities even out, and what emerges is a fair picture of a player's performance relative to others playing in the same season.

Have you ever asked yourself, since baseball games are decided by runs alone, why bother to keep laborious records of hits, errors, assists—not to mention such minutiae of play as intentional walks, passed balls, sacrifice flies? After all, at the office picnic softball game, all we do is keep track of the runs, and players and spectators alike have fun. And besides, it must have been that way when the game was first developed.

Heresy? Yes, of course, heresy. And I would not spend two seconds on the rack to defend it. It was the genius of Henry Chadwick, the earliest known codifier of playing rules and keeper of game records, the inventor of that masterpiece of recapitulation, the box score, to recognize that a record of the performance of each player and the degree to which he contributed to victory (or defeat) would add measurably to the pleasure of watching the sport. It would be hard to imagine any sport today maintaining mass appeal without being accompanied by exhaustive records of individual performance.

Born in Exeter, England, in 1824, son of a British journalist and sportsman, Chadwick was brought by his family to Brooklyn at the age of thirteen and spent the remainder of his life there. (How much of baseball history is associated with that much maligned borough and what a shame that it no longer has a team.) He died in 1908, by that time known almost universally as the "Father of Baseball" and mourned by a baseball establishment that his influence on playing rules had helped to create.

There is a story that Chadwick, who almost certainly knew both cricket and rounders from his boyhood in England, was covering a cricket match in Jersey City in the 1850s for a New York newspaper when his attention was drawn to some young men playing the new game of baseball in an adjacent field. There was something about the tempo and style of the game that attracted him, and he made it a point to learn more about it. There is a tradition, too, that in his brief playing career he was a shortstop. If true, it may account for the fact that later in life he was known as a devotee of good fielding.

In time, Chadwick entered his father's profession of journalism full-time, and as a fluent and enthusiastic reporter on baseball activities in Brooklyn and New York City, he virtually created the role of the baseball writer. It was from this vantage point that he came to have a profound influence on the ultimate adoption by organized baseball of uniform scoring rules. Beginning in the 1870s, he became a familiar figure at all professional games in the New York City area, dignified, bearded, wearing a frock coat and stovepipe hat, and never without his big, black scorebook. It is reported that small boys would nudge one another and whisper, "There's the guy who invented baseball."

The evolution of the function of the official scorer is not

absolutely clear, although it is certain that Chadwick had an important role in it if for no other reason than that he was instrumental in the formation of the Baseball Writers Association of America (BBWAA), whose members took on the responsibility for scoring for most of the present century.

In the so-called amateur era—through the 1860s—the scorer and the umpire seemed to be one and the same, an intolerable situation when you think about it, since he could hardly have done either job very well. The functions were separated before the adoption of uniform rules, and you even begin to see a division between the scoring rules and the rules of the game. Aside from whatever direct influence Chadwick might have had, it is not surprising that the task of keeping a comprehensive record should have been turned over to reporters who regularly covered the games. To report the results adequately for their readers, they had to keep some kind of record of the action anyway. And they must have understood baseball, or they would not have been regularly assigned to cover it.

The official scorer has a lot more to do than make judgment calls on hits and errors, although it may be by that function that he is best known to the average fan. Under the official rules and by appointment from the league president, the official scorer must keep an exact and accurate record of everything that happens in a league championship game. Everything. That means the number of assists by each fielder, the number of sacrifice hits by each batter, the number of walks that were intentional, the exact playing time of the game with interruptions like rain delays subtracted, the list goes on. There is no one else gathering this information *officially*, although today especially there are other agents, such as statisticians for TV networks, who keep track of the action for their own purposes.

When the scorer has made a record of all this—and, incidentally, tried to watch the game at the same time— he must enter it on an elaborate report form prescribed by the league president, prove the box score to account for every base achieved in the game, and forward the report to the league office within thirty-six hours of the end of the game. For this the official scorer is paid fifty dollars by the league, although he is not considered a league employee. Not long ago the honorarium was a lot less than that. The scorers can't have been doing it for the money.

How can some guy with thick glasses sitting up in the press box, his hands full trying to keep track of the number of fielder's choices and do a story for his newspaper, tell what's a hit and what's an error, especially when he's never been on a big-league diamond, looking down the barrel at a Jim Rice or an Eddie Murray? Well, when the baseball writers were doing the scoring exclusively, the qualifications were fairly formidable: five years' experience on a regular baseball beat and attendance at a hundred games or more a season, which meant that you had to be traveling with the team. Besides, anyone writing about baseball has had a glove on at some time in his life and understands what ordinary effort is. Blake Cullen of the National League office says, "The best people to score are those who watch from the press box level and have a feel for it. It's really just a question of seeing enough games and knowing what's going on."

In recent years, for one reason or another, fewer newspapers have been willing to permit their writers to act as scorers. This fact coupled with the decline in the number of big-city dailies has seriously reduced the pool of qualified scorers. The leagues have been making use of retired baseball writers, college coaches, and others they feel are well qualified, but the situation has revived recommendations that baseball establish a corps of official scorers under the tutelage of a league supervisor, just as they operate a corps of umpires. Both leagues agree that they are probably going to move in that direction, although no firm decision has been made yet.

I don't know when it first occurred to someone that the system of compiling putouts, assists, and errors is not the most satisfactory measure of a fielder's ability. Possibly shortly after the system was devised. It has long been the custom among both writers and fans to make their own evaluations from what they see on the field. It's what I call the Herman Long-Zeke Bonura corollary. Long made a ton of errors, but everyone who watched him agreed that he was a good fielder. And Zeke . . .

The problem arises from the scoring rules themselves as much as from the ways in which they are applied by the official scorer. Every fan is familiar with the cheap hits that accumulate when lethargic or inept outfielders don't get a jump on the ball or when a pop fly falls for a double amidst three momentarily paralyzed fielders, called the Alphonse and Gaston act. Add to that the ground balls that skip by infielders possessed of little or no lateral movement. Under the present rules, the scorer must award a hit in these cases. He has no other choice.

For many years, Dick Young of the New York *Daily News* has lobbied for the adoption of the team error for plays on which there has obviously been sloppy fielding but where the miscue can't be justifiably charged to a single player, as in the Alphonse and Gaston situation. He argues that it would cut down on the cheap hits and over the course of a season would tell something about how well drilled a team was in its defense.

Allen Lewis, for a dozen years chairman of the scoring-rules committee, is adamantly opposed to the team-error idea. "If you put in team errors," he says, "you know

what's going to happen? They're going to blame everything on a team error. It would become a catchall for plays
that the scorer didn't want to make a tough decision on.
You can't reduce baseball to black and white. If you play a
hundred and sixty-two games, that stuff evens out."

Former *New York Post* writer Leonard Koppett, now
on the Stanford University faculty, not only supports the
idea of a team error, but also proposes a "constitutional
convention" on scoring rules, which would deal with such
problems as how to distinguish between the hard and easy
chance in the field.

When he was writing for the old *Washington Star*, Jack
Mann used to kid about what he called Mann's Law: two is
greater than one. "Call an error and you displease the batter and the fielder," he wrote. "Call a hit and you displease only the pitcher. Therefore . . ." In the days when
a player was paid solely for his offensive ability, it was
probably harmless to affect a cavalier attitude toward
fielding. Now that it seems evident that some clubs are
willing to pay big salaries to players who offer top gloves
but not much offense, the situation calls for a long hard
look at how we evaluate fielding for the record.

Since the scoring rules were made uniform in the 1870s,
when batting average was the sole criterion of a batter's
worth, a number of additional measurements have won official recognition—runs scored, runs batted in, extra-base
hits, primarily home runs, total bases, slugging average,
bases on balls, stolen bases, on-base percentage, and,
most recently, game-winning RBIs. It is curious, when
you stop to think about it, that in the same period, double
plays participated in and total chances per game are the
only things we have, in addition to the traditional putouts,
assists, errors, and fielding average, as measures of fielding skill.

The Gold Glove Award has been a commendable move by an unofficial agency to call attention to the deficiencies in the way that organized baseball evaluates fielding for the record. But Gold Glove itself is totally subjective and recognizes just one fielder at each position in each league.

In an effort to deal systematically with such nebulous skills as range, Bill James in his *Baseball Abstract* uses a complex formula to arrive at a player's defensive won/lost percentage, which is keyed to a team's success or failure. The criteria vary from position to position and incorporate such factors as fielding average, double plays participated in, range index, and the number of games the player has been in. I don't doubt that James's formula offers a better measure of defensive effectiveness than does fielding average alone, but for the average fan it may be a bit too complicated for fullest appreciation. James is currently gathering game records with the help of volunteers in every major-league city in what he calls Project Scoresheet, which should yield, along with an abundance of other stats, a measure called "defensive innings." It might prove very valuable in expanding the fan's appreciation for the defensive skills of individual players.

Craig Wright, SABRmetrician for the Texas Rangers, has devised his own formula for rating defensive skills by position, one which compares a player with others who play the same position in his league. Wright's system is used within the Ranger organization, but has no official status outside of it. It has yielded such surprising results as Detroit's Chet Lemon's 4.04 advantage over the Yankees' Gold Glove winner Dave Winfield (a very wide margin according to the system).

I asked Wright whether he thought the leagues would soon begin to adopt officially some of the new formulas for measuring defensive skills. "Probably not," he said. "Baseball's a traditional game and that's one of its triumphs. Fielding percentage is going to be with us until the day we die."

ELEVEN
The Purest Gold

"They flash upon that inward eye which is the bliss of solitude."
— WILLIAM WORDSWORTH

WHEN I STARTED THIS BOOK I PLEDGED MYself not to succumb to temptation and name an all-time fielding team. That resolve proved to have about as much iron as my annual decision to give up Twinkies and lose weight. Maybe it was all those weeks spent reviewing accounts from the past of great catches and throws to the plate. Or possibly the involuntary reliving of the portions of my life so agreeably idled away at the ball park. All I know is that the urge to pontificate has become too powerful to be denied.

Putting together fantasy teams is not only pleasurable, it is easy. You say to yourself, which pitcher should I start today, Mathewson or Spahn? No, let's make that Lefty Grove. If I had to choose the best fielding team that I actually saw perform, it would be quite another matter. The formidable Baltimore Orioles of 1969–70 come to mind. Or some of the Chicago White Sox teams of the mid-1950s. Forced to a decision, I would have to say the 1952 Brooklyn Dodgers, Roger Kahn's Boys of Summer.

What a lineup. Not a doubtful glove in sight. Gil Hodges at first, Jackie Robinson at second, Billy Cox at third, Pee Wee Reese at short, Andy Pafko in left, Duke Snider in center, Carl Furillo in right, and Campanella behind the plate. Greatest collection of arms I've ever seen, too.

But back to fantasy. I have set two limitations on my choices. They include only players that I have seen a reasonable number of times and only men who are already retired.

Pitcher—Bob Gibson. "Boileryard" Clarke, a catcher with the famous Baltimore Orioles of John McGraw's day and for thirty years after his playing days baseball coach at Princeton, once commented that "few conditions are more fatal to a ball team than that of having weak-fielding pitchers." It's a view that few would challenge, and yet every week big-league teams run into trouble because a pitcher has failed to carry out his fielding assignment. The pitcher has just a few set plays to worry about: fielding the medium-strength bunt to either side of the mound, the sharp comebacker, and covering first on balls hit at the first baseman. They are not easy, any of them, and they must be executed perfectly.

There may have been hundreds of pitchers over the years who learned to field their position close to perfection. Names like Walter Johnson, Artie Nehf, Fred Fitzsimmons, Burleigh Grimes, Pete Alexander, Claude Passeau, Bob Lemon, and Bucky Walters are most likely to come up in discussions of great-fielding pitchers. More recently, Jim Kaat won sixteen consecutive Gold Gloves, and I guess that Jim had few peers at moving to his right off the mound. But I want Bob Gibson on my team. I want him because he was the consummate athlete and competitor, and it's the contingency plays, not the set ones, that are most likely to cost you a championship.

In a regular season game in July 1964, Gibson had his leg broken by a line drive back through the box. His first reaction was not to cradle the shattered limb, but to throw out the batter. That illustrates why I want him on the mound for my team.

Catcher—Johnny Bench. Johnny made the choice of catcher easier for me by retiring after the 1983 season. Otherwise, I might have spent hours, even days, weighing the records of Mickey Cochrane, Bill Dickey, Jim Hegan, Johnny Edwards, and possibly a few others, and replaying in my mind recollections of big, graceful men shifting behind the plate to block wild pitches, throwing out runners, and plucking pop fouls off the screen.

I have watched Bench more recently than I have the others, and I am satisfied in my mind that he made every play you could expect from a catcher with an ease and precision that may have been matched at times, but never exceeded. I have never seen a stronger arm on a catcher.

First base—Bill Terry. Call this a sentimental choice if you will. I have convinced myself that it is an honest one. It's quite possible that I didn't get to see enough of Vic Power or Charlie Grimm or Gil Hodges or Mickey Vernon or Bill White. Maybe I wasn't watching closely enough when I did see them play. To salve my conscience, I com-

pared notes with a few old-timers, including Paul Mac
Farlane. Their comments helped reinforce my conviction
that if the World Series hung in the balance and one of my
infielders uncorked a throw into the dirt on a close play, I
would want Terry on first.

Second base—Bill Mazeroski. This may have been the
toughest choice. Sentimentally, I lean toward Charlie
Gehringer, the most graceful second baseman I have ever
seen. I have always admired the absolute concentration of
Joe Morgan. But Joe was so totally the child of Astroturf
through his long career at the Astrodome, Riverfront, and
the Vet that we may never know how great he really was
with the glove.

I turned the name of Bobby Doerr over in my mind
more than a few times. Fans under fifty will not remember Bobby, but let me assure you that he was a marvel at anything a second baseman is expected to do.

In the final analysis I was won over by Maz's energetic
style, his workhorse qualities, and most of all by his wizardry at turning the double play. The older baseball gets,
the larger the double play seems to loom in defense. In his
book on strategy, Earl Weaver says plainly that the main
function of a second baseman and a shortstop is to turn
the double play. The real test of a defense is the ability to
kill rallies.

I could not help recollecting, too, that Mazeroski had to
play for years alongside first basemen like Dick Stuart and
Donn Clendenon. That means that Maz's effective range
had to be from second base to the foul line.

Third base—Brooks Robinson. For anyone who ever
saw Brooks play third—and he has been retired almost
eight years now, incredible as that seems—it should not
be necessary to defend the choice. I have heard some good
third basemen charged with being unnecessarily flam-

boyant in their play. Not Brooks Robinson. It seemed to me that for all the dazzling stops he made, especially in big games, he never generated any fireworks that didn't grow directly out of the nature of the play. Hardworking, self-effacing, brilliant.

Shortstop—Luis Aparicio. "Little Looie" played more than 2,500 American League games at shortstop, a major-league record. No active shortstop is even close. It seemed to a lot of observers that Aparicio was moving just as fast at the end as on the day he reported to Comiskey Park back in 1956. Common sense suggests that this is sentimental illusion. But it says something about the impression made during almost two decades of gathering up everything in sight with his darting moves and cutting down thousands of runners with his quick release.

Aparicio participated in 1,553 double plays, a major-league record. When I think of him hooked up with Mazeroski, all I can see is empty bases. I ran replays of half a dozen of my favorite shortstops past the inner eye, but my choice always returned to Luis. For speed, style, and efficiency, I have seen none better.

Left field—Joe DiMaggio. Yes, I fudged on this one. Imagine anyone having the temerity to put one of history's greatest center fielders in left. It's the dilemma of the child in the candy shop. I want both Joe and Willie Mays in my outfield and, by George, since this is fantasy, I shall have them. The fact is that Joe did play left field when he first reported to the Yankees, though not for long.

If driven into a corner on this one, I will accept Yastrzemski as a replacement, not exactly what you would call a hardship. It's common for managers to shift outfielders around these days. Finding a "pure" left fielder like Zack Wheat in the modern game is difficult. Let me have DiMag.

Center field—Willie Mays. I chose Mays over DiMaggio in center because he was faster and was able to play shallower. I have never seen an outfielder with greater range than Mays had. No one ever played the impossibly deep center field at the Polo Grounds as well.

Neither Mays nor DiMaggio put any fielding records in the book. But no two outfielders in history seemed so innately qualified to make the really big play, the one that saves championships. When Willie made his famous catch against Vic Wertz in 1954, the Indians had two on and none out in the eighth inning of a tie game. They failed to score and the Giants won in the tenth inning. There's more than chance involved here. That's why I want Willie.

Right field—Roberto Clemente. I spent a couple of hours pacing the floor mumbling Ott, Clemente, Ott, Clemente. Clemente was the faster of the two, though neither could have stayed within Rickey Henderson's shadow in a ten-yard dash. They both had enough speed to cover right field with something to spare. Mel may have had a slightly more accurate arm, though here we are splitting hairs. Bobby was the more aggressive fielder, probably took more chances. In a very close decision I must go with Clemente.

What I liked best about Clemente is the same thing I liked about DiMaggio and Mays, the capacity to make the big play at the most pressing time. There was, for example, a throw in the 1971 World Series, which I can still see in my mind but can't fix exactly. I am only sure that it was in the seventh game. With a runner on second, representing the tying run, a Baltimore batter flied to Clemente in medium-deep right. After the catch, he unleashed a cannon shot to third and the Orioles were dissuaded from sending the runner. As a consequence of their inability to advance the runner to third, Baltimore failed to score, lost the game, and with it the Series.

There they are. Any of you gap hitters ready to bat
against this crew?

p Gibson
c Bench
1b Terry
2b Mazeroski
3b Robinson
ss Aparicio
lf DiMaggio
cf Mays
rf Clemente

I am ashamed to admit that such a thought crossed my
mind while I was in the act of compiling an all-time defensive team, but any Old Testament prophet could have told
you that the naughtiest, most pleasure-laden thoughts are
the most difficult to banish. This collection of defensive
wizards could also hit. I took the trouble to add up the
numbers. A team lifetime batting average of .289 sounds
impressive to me. And 2,292 homers. Even Gibson had 24.
Bring on the 1927 Yankees.

Index

231